MY **REVISION** NOTES

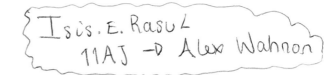

Pearson Edexcel

GCSE (9-1)

MIGRANTS IN BRITAIN

c800–PRESENT & NOTTING HILL, c1948–c1970

Sam Slater

HODDER
EDUCATION
AN HACHETTE UK COMPANY

The Publishers would like to thank the following for permission to reproduce copyright material.

Photo credits

p.33 © George W. Hales/Fox Photos/Getty Images; **p.35** © Knoote/Daily Express/Hulton Archive/Getty Images; **p.42** © Charlie Phillips/Getty Images

Acknowledgements

Every effort has been made to trace all copyright holders, but if any have been inadvertently overlooked, the Publishers will be pleased to make the necessary arrangements at the first opportunity.

Although every effort has been made to ensure that website addresses are correct at time of going to press, Hodder Education cannot be held responsible for the content of any website mentioned in this book. It is sometimes possible to find a relocated web page by typing in the address of the home page for a website in the URL window of your browser.

Hachette UK's policy is to use papers that are natural, renewable and recyclable products and made from wood grown in well-managed forests and other controlled sources. The logging and manufacturing processes are expected to conform to the environmental regulations of the country of origin.

Orders: please contact Hachette UK Distribution, Hely Hutchinson Centre, Milton Road, Didcot, Oxfordshire, OX11 7HH. Telephone: +44 (0)1235 827827. Email education@hachette.co.uk Lines are open from 9 a.m. to 5 p.m., Monday to Friday. You can also order through our website: www.hoddereducation.co.uk

ISBN: 9781398368187

First published in 2022 by
Hodder Education,
An Hachette UK Company
Carmelite House
50 Victoria Embankment
London EC4Y 0DZ

www.hoddereducation.co.uk

Impression number   10 9 8 7 6 5 4 3 2

Year   2026 2025 2024 2023

Cover photo © Trinity Mirror / Mirrorpix / Alamy Stock Photo

Illustrations by Aptara Inc.

Typeset in India by Aptara Inc.

Printed in the UK

A catalogue record for this title is available from the British Library.

How to get the most out of this book

This book will help you revise for the thematic study and historic environment: Migrants in Britain, c.800–present and Notting Hill, c.1948–c.1970.

The content in the book is organised into a series of double-page spreads which cover the content in the specification. The left-hand page on each spread has the key content for each topic, and the right-hand page has one or two activities to help you with exam skills or to learn the knowledge you need. Answers to these activities can be found online at www.hoddereducation.co.uk/myrevisionnotes. Quick multiple-choice quizzes to test your knowledge of each topic can be found there too.

At the end of the book is an exam focus section (pages 40–46) which gives you guidance on how to answer each exam question type.

Tick to track your progress

You can also keep track of your revision by ticking off each topic heading in the book. You may find it helpful to add your own notes as you work through each topic.

Use the revision planner on pages 2–3 to track your progress, topic by topic. Tick each box when you have:

1 revised and understood each topic
2 completed the activities
3 checked your answers online.

Features to help you succeed

Key terms

Key terms are highlighted in blue the first time they appear, with an explanation nearby in the margin. As you work through this book, highlight other key ideas and add your own notes. Make this your book.

Exam tips

Throughout the book there are exam tips that remind you of key points that will help you in the exam.

Revision tasks

Shorter revision tasks help you remember key points of content.

Activities

There are a variety of activities for you to complete related to the content on the left-hand page. Some are based on exam-style questions which aim to consolidate your revision and practise your exam skills. Others are revision tasks to make sure that you have understood every topic and to help you record the key information about each topic.

My revision planner

Check your understanding and progress at **www.hoddereducation.co.uk/myrevisionnotes**

Key topic 4: c.1900–present: Migration in modern Britain

Part 2: Notting Hill, c.1948–c.1970

Exam focus

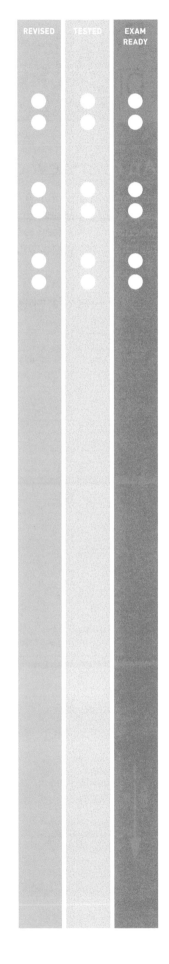

My revision planner

REVISED   TESTED   EXAM READY

3

Part 1: Migrants in Britain, c.800–present

An overview of migration from c.800

Migrants in Britain is a development study. It is important that you have a secure chronological understanding of the content – what happened, and when. You also need to be able to identify change and continuity in the reasons for migration, experience of migrants and the impact of migrants.

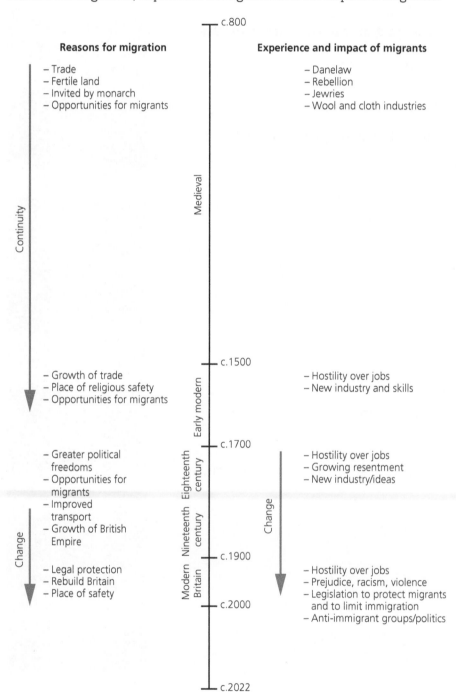

Reasons for migration

- Trade
- Fertile land
- Invited by monarch
- Opportunities for migrants

Continuity

- Growth of trade
- Place of religious safety
- Opportunities for migrants

- Greater political freedoms
- Opportunities for migrants
- Improved transport
- Growth of British Empire

Change

- Legal protection
- Rebuild Britain
- Place of safety

c.800

Medieval

c.1500

Early modern

c.1700

Eighteenth century

Nineteenth century

Modern Britain

c.1900

c.2000

c.2022

Experience and impact of migrants

- Danelaw
- Rebellion
- Jewries
- Wool and cloth industries

- Hostility over jobs
- New industry and skills

- Hostility over jobs
- Growing resentment
- New industry/ideas

Change

- Hostility over jobs
- Prejudice, racism, violence
- Legislation to protect migrants and to limit immigration
- Anti-immigrant groups/politics

Check your understanding and progress at **www.hoddereducation.co.uk/myrevisionnotes**

Factors in migration

Factors are things that influenced migration in the following ways:
+ They helped to cause change: for example, the factor of attitudes in society led to discrimination towards Jewish migrants in medieval England.
+ They helped to prevent change: for example, the factor of economic influences continued to attract migrants to Britain from c.800 to the present day.

The main factors that you could be asked about in your exam are shown in the diagram below, with an explanation of what they mean.

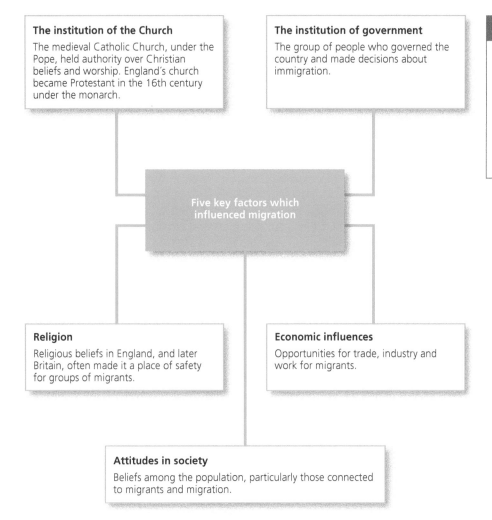

The institution of the Church
The medieval Catholic Church, under the Pope, held authority over Christian beliefs and worship. England's church became Protestant in the 16th century under the monarch.

The institution of government
The group of people who governed the country and made decisions about immigration.

Five key factors which influenced migration

Religion
Religious beliefs in England, and later Britain, often made it a place of safety for groups of migrants.

Economic influences
Opportunities for trade, industry and work for migrants.

Attitudes in society
Beliefs among the population, particularly those connected to migrants and migration.

> **Exam tip**
>
> You need to be able to explain what each factor is and how each factor contributed to migration in Britain since c.800. Look at what factors caused change and continuity. Look for patterns and trends.

> **Revision task**
>
> Create a table of the factors in each time period that led to a change in the reasons for migration to Britain, and the experiences and impact of migrants in Britain since c.800.

Key topic 1: c.800–c.1500: Migration in medieval England

1 The context for migration

1.1 The context of English society

REVISED ○

The growth of towns and the economic opportunities they provided played a significant role in the reasons for migration to England during this period.

Medieval England attracted migrants for the following reasons:

Land ownership and the growth of towns
As trade throughout England increased, towns grew, including York, St Ives and Northampton.

The role of the wool industry
English wool, woven into cloth, was highly sought after across Europe. Exports increased throughout the medieval period.

Reasons for migration and patterns of settlement

Opportunities for migrants
Migrants were attracted to the job opportunities, such as weaving cloth, in English towns as trade increased.

The role of the monarchy
Monarchs invited groups of migrants to England when they needed their skills for managing royal finance and to start a cloth industry.

England as a part of Christendom
Medieval Christians felt united by the authority of the Pope and the universal Church. Monks from France were encouraged to migrate to England by the Normans. Church services and holy books were in Latin.

Key terms

Christendom The realms where Christianity was the dominant faith

Vikings People from Scandinavian countries such as Norway, Sweden and Denmark

Fertile (Land that was) capable of being farmed for food

Danelaw The part of England where the laws of the Vikings dominated

Normandy A dukedom in north-west France

Charter A written grant by a monarch that outlines the rights of a city

Low Countries A region of north-west Europe that included Belgium, the Netherlands and Luxembourg

1.2 Reasons for migration and patterns of settlement

REVISED ○

Various migrant groups were attracted to England during the years c.800 to c.1500 for different reasons:

Migrant group	Reasons for migration
Vikings	The first Viking raid on England took place in 789. More raids followed as Vikings searched for valuable items such as gold, silver and jewels in monasteries and abbeys. By the ninth century, the Vikings wanted to invade England to settle and farm the lush, fertile land and become rich from the trade already established with Europe from English towns. In 866 the Vikings captured the city of York. From York, they went on to conquer most of eastern England. This territory became known as the Danelaw. As Viking settlements expanded, their families joined them as farmers, workers and traders.
Normans	Led by William, Duke of Normandy, the Normans invaded England in 1066. William believed he had been promised the crown by the late King, Edward the Confessor. William was able to extend his power and the Normans that followed him became rich from owning the land. William appointed Lanfranc as Archbishop of Canterbury in 1070. Lanfranc went on to appoint Norman migrants and Cluniac monks to senior positions, such as bishops, in the English Church.
Jewish people	In the 1070s, King William I invited a group of Jewish merchants from Normandy to England, to learn from their main experience and skill of making money (as Catholics were forbidden to lend money and gain interest). At first, they lent money to William, and went on to share in his increased wealth. Jewish migrants settled in places such as London, Canterbury and York. After 1135, more Jewish families migrated to England as towns and trade grew. By the mid-thirteenth century, there were Jewish communities in many English towns.
Other European traders and craftsmen	England was a successful centre for trade throughout the medieval period. European traders and craftsmen settled in English towns to organise their trade with Europe. From the twelfth century, English rulers encouraged trade by issuing charters to towns, which allowed them to hold annual fairs. Migrants from the Low Countries were attracted to English towns where they were given work. Weavers were attracted to England by the wool industry. In 1331, weavers from the Low Countries were invited to England by Edward III to weave cloth from English wool, which was then sold at high prices.

Key factors

Institutions (Government) Monarchs, including King William I and King Henry III, invited groups of migrants to England to support their governance and increase royal finance.

Institutions (the Church) Norman migrants, including the Cluniac monks and Cistercians, were appointed to senior positions in the English Church by Lanfranc.

Economic influences Many groups of migrants were attracted to England for work opportunities in the towns, especially as weavers.

Exam tip

The Vikings and Normans migrated to England because they were invaders. This is unique to the years c.800–c.1100.

Complete the paragraph

Below is an exam-style question and a paragraph which is part of an answer to this question. The paragraph gives a reason for the continuity in reasons for migration to England and some historical support, but does not go on to develop the explanation.

1   Rewrite the paragraph with extra, precise, supporting knowledge and a full explanation linking back to the question.

2   Complete the answer to this question:

   Explain why there was continuity in the reasons for migration to England during the period c.800–c.1500. (12 marks)

> You may use the following in your answer:
> + The monarchy   + The wool industry
>
> You **must** also use information of your own.

During the years c.800 to c.1500 people continued to migrate to England because they were invited by the ruling monarch. In 1070, King William I invited a group of Jewish merchants from Normandy to England. In Normandy, these Jewish merchants had demonstrated their skills in finance (as Catholics were forbidden to lend money and gain interest) and William wanted to learn from them to increase his wealth in England. Initially, the Jewish merchants lent money to William, but they later benefited from his financial investments.

2 The experience and impact of migrants

Migrants had a range of positive and negative experiences between c.800 and c.1500. All migrants in England have had some kind of impact ever since.

2.1 The experience of migrants in England

Vikings

Evidence suggests that the Viking migrants, soon called Danes, and the Saxons (who already lived there) adapted to each other and lived peacefully. Many Danes became Christians. Others continued to worship their own gods.

Saxon rulers continued to fight the Danes in the South however. In 1016, the Saxons surrendered, and Cnut (or Canute) became king of England. King Cnut:

+ allowed Saxons to hold power
+ supported the Christian church and worked with the Pope to increase England's importance in Christendom
+ used Danegeld to prevent any further Viking raids.

Normans

After the Battle of Hastings (1066), Norman migrants faced a series of rebellions. They gained control by building castles and cathedrals, creating fear from the Harrying of the North, and introducing the feudal system.

Jewish people

For many years Jewish migrants were accepted because their money and skills in finance helped businesses and trade to be successful, although of course some Jewish people were poor, just like some Saxons and Normans. Jewish families settled in separate areas called Jewries. They wanted to live near people who shared their beliefs and customs.

Antisemitism already existed but became more evident in England in the twelfth and thirteenth centuries:

+ Jewish people could pay to shelter in royal castles during times of crisis. To pay for this, they charged higher interest rates, which caused resentment.
+ Jewish people were the only non-Christian group, which caused unfair suspicion.
+ In 1190, all Jewish people in York were killed in the Cliffords Tower massacre.
+ In 1218, Jewish people were forced to wear a yellow cloth patch for identification.
+ In the 1230s, Jewish people were expelled from towns such as Leicester and Newcastle.

From 1265, the Pope allowed Italian bankers to charge interest on loans. They migrated to England, and so English kings became less reliant on Jewish people for money and less willing to protect them. In 1275, King Edward I banned them from collecting interest and left them very poor. In 1290, all Jewish people were ordered to convert to Christianity or leave England. Most chose to leave.

Other European traders and craftsmen

Flemish bricklayers and Dutch brewers taught the English new skills and techniques. The success of the cloth industry, helped by Flemish weavers, benefited England due to the increase in demand for woven wool.

From the thirteenth century, families with experience and skills in banking moved to London. They lent money to English kings, and were given royal protection and more advantages to trade in wool.

Key terms

Danegeld Money paid to the Danes to stop them invading England

Harrying of the North Between 1069 and 1070 the Normans took revenge on the North following a series of rebellions by burning crops, killing livestock and destroying homes

Feudal system A system introduced by King William where he lent land throughout England in return for loyalty

Antisemitism Hostility or prejudice against Jewish people

Exam tip

When you are asked to consider the impact of different migrant groups, think about the changes that took place because of their presence. Don't describe their migration – try to explain the consequences of their migration instead.

Revision task

Create a mind map of the ways that migrants impacted on England in the years c.800 to c.1500. You could organise your mind map with a separate leg for each migrant group.

Check your understanding and progress at **www.hoddereducation.co.uk/myrevisionnotes**

From 1303, German Hansa merchants were given the right to trade timber, furs and honey, as well as receiving royal protection and lower tax rates than other merchants. By the fifteenth century, they controlled most of the English cloth export trade. The Black Death (1348) caused many deaths, so migrants were welcomed.

From 1378, denization was introduced.

However, European migrants were not always welcomed:

+ Many English craftsmen believed European migrants were taking their jobs and ruining their trade.
+ During the Peasants Revolt (1381), about 150 European weavers and merchants were murdered.

+ During times of conflict, such as 1381, the English attacked Hansa merchants. Migrant groups were seen as the 'alien' and treated with suspicion and fear because it was believed they could side with, and help, the enemy.

Key terms

Denization Favoured wealthy migrants were allowed to swear an oath of allegiance to the monarch and, in return, secure the same legal rights as English-born citizens

Peasants Revolt In 1381, thousands of English peasants demanded freedom from their lords and higher wages

Norse The Viking language

2.2 The impact of migrants in England

REVISED

Danelaw	The basis of Viking law-making was 'do not kill' and 'do not steal', both of which continue to today.
Culture (religion, language)	The Vikings (Danes) spoke Old Norse. Modern English contains many Old Norse words, such as 'smile' and 'knife'.
	The Normans spoke Old French. Gradually it was combined with the English language spoken by Saxons and words such as 'beef' and 'pork' emerged. Norman names, such as Robert and William, have continued to today.
	The Normans changed the Church when William replaced all but one of the Saxon bishops with Norman ones. Links with Christendom grew as members of religious orders migrated to England, founding monasteries and abbeys.
Trade	Jewish migrants lent money to people starting businesses in England, and to merchants overseas.
	Migrants from Europe in the fourteenth and fifteenth centuries changed England's economy. A new system developed where raw materials, such as wool, became manufactured goods, such as cloth, which could be traded. England became a key trading centre because of migrants.
The built environment	The Normans changed the English landscape by building castles and cathedrals. William I built castles, including the Tower of London, with money lent by Jewish migrants. Later, Henry III obtained money unfairly from Jewish financiers to rebuild Westminster Abbey.

Support or challenge

Below is an exam-style question which asks how far you agree with a specific statement. Below this are a series of general statements which are relevant to the question. Using the information on pages 8–9 and your own knowledge, decide whether these statements support or challenge the statement in the question and tick the appropriate box.

'The most significant impact of migrants in medieval England between c.800 and c.1500 was on trade.' How far do you agree? Explain your answer. (16 marks, with a further 4 marks available for spelling, punctuation and grammar.)

You may use the following in your answer:
+ Wool industry
+ Castles

You **must** also use some information of your own.

Statement	Support	Challenge
The basis of Viking law-making was 'do not kill' and 'do not steal'.		
The Normans changed the landscape of England by building castles and cathedrals.		
Jewish people in Oxford played a significant part in establishing the university, especially Merton College.		
Jewish migrants lent money to merchants to expand their trade overseas.		
England became a key trading centre of woollen cloth.		

Once you have completed this table, write an answer to the question.

3 Case study

3.1 The city of York under the Vikings

REVISED ⬤

In 866, the Vikings conquered Northumbria and captured York. They changed the name of York to Jorvik. York is located where the rivers Ouse and Foss meet. It is also located at the centre of a large network of Roman roads.

The city of York grew fast under the Vikings. Historians estimate that between 10,000 and 15,000 people migrated to York from abroad and within England between 866 and 950.

Reasons for migration and settlement

York was important to the Vikings because it was:

+ the capital of the northern kingdom of Northumbria, which made it central to northern governance and trade
+ a wealthy city
+ the only city in the north with its own mint
+ located at the centre of a road and river network which made transportation and trading easier
+ full of fertile soil for farming.

Experiences of Viking migrants

Evidence suggests that the Vikings lived peacefully alongside other inhabitants of York. The first Vikings were pagans, and little is known about their religion. However, there is evidence that the Vikings accepted the Christian religion of the Anglo-Saxon people. Some Viking kings converted to Christianity and some Viking rulers were buried in York Minster, the centre of Christianity in the north. There was conflict between the Vikings and Anglo-Saxon kingdoms in the south over territory as the Vikings tried to extend their influence.

Impact of Viking migration

Evidence of the impact of the Viking settlement in York has come from archaeological digs. These digs have shown the wealth of the city of York during the Viking settlement. Archaeologists have shown that:

+ York became a multicultural city; Northumbrians and Vikings lived alongside workers and merchants from Germany, Ireland and Scotland
+ York became a centre of trade and wealth. People worked as blacksmiths and jewellery-makers, and with textiles, pottery, glass recycling and metals
+ York attracted trade from across England, such as tin from Cornwall, and across Europe, such as amber from the Baltic Sea region, Hone stone from Scandinavia, and gold and silver from Europe and Ireland
+ Viking coins have been found across England, which shows that they traded with the rest of the country
+ hunting and farming took place on the fertile land around York, which also enabled the Vikings to increase their wealth
+ Viking place names were used in the city of York, such as 'gate' which is Norse for 'street'.

Key migrant group

Vikings People from the Scandinavian countries of Norway, Sweden and Denmark. The Vikings settled in England from 865

Key terms

Mint A place where coins are produced under government authority

Pagan A person who held religious beliefs other than those of the main world religions

---

Key factors

Economic influences Trade was the key reason for the Viking migration to York, and central to the impact that the Vikings had on the city and England.

Exam tip

When you revise the migration of Vikings to York, consider:

+ their reasons for migration to York
+ their experience in York
+ their impact on the city of York.

Organising knowledge

Use the information on page 10 to complete the table below to categorise the migration of Vikings to the city of York.

Reasons for migration and patterns of settlement	The experience of Vikings in the city of York	The impact of Vikings on the city of York

Analysing factors

You need to understand the role that factors had on the Viking migration to England. Copy and complete the diagram below. For each factor in the diagram, explain how it influenced the city of York under the Vikings. If a factor contributed in multiple ways, you need to have more than one explanation.

Once you have completed the diagram, decide which factor you think was the most significant and why. For a reminder about each factor, see page 5.

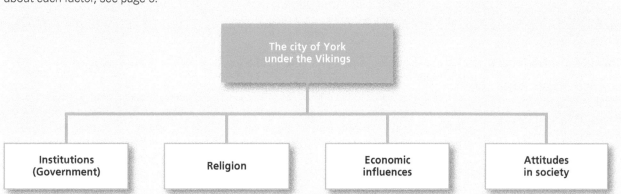

The city of York under the Vikings

- Institutions (Government)
- Religion
- Economic influences
- Attitudes in society

Key topic 2: c.1500–c.1700: Migration in early modern England

1 The context for migration

1.1 The changing context of English society

The years c.1500 to c.1700 brought great changes to England, which had a large impact on migration.

Changes in religion	
England was seen as a place of safety for Protestants during these years. Non-Catholics migrated to England to avoid persecution.	In 1500, England was a Catholic country under the Pope. In 1534 Henry VIII made himself head of the Church in England instead. Protestant ideas influenced changes and then: ✦ when Edward VI (1547–53) ruled, England became a Protestant country ✦ when Mary I (1553–58) ruled, England returned to being a Catholic country ✦ finally, when Elizabeth I (1558–1603) ruled, England became a fully Protestant country.
Changes in government	
Government was closely linked to religion. The Protestant governments welcomed European Protestants to England as a humanitarian and economic act.	During the 1500s, Parliament was called more regularly and played a greater role in England's affairs. In the 1600s: ✦ Parliament's belief that it should control the government led to the English Civil War between 1642 and 1651. King Charles I was executed in 1649 and Oliver Cromwell ruled England as a republic for 11 years ✦ Parliament invited King Charles II to return in 1660, but his powers were limited ✦ James II became king in 1685 but he was very unpopular because he was Catholic. As a result, Parliament invited the Protestant Prince William of Orange and his wife Mary to 'invade' England and become joint monarchs. Mary was James II's daughter.
Changes in global trade	
The growth in trade led some Indian people, mainly sailors and servants, to migrate to England. The growth of the British Empire began the forced migration of enslaved African people to England's colonies, and, by 1700, to England.	Between the years c.1500 and c.1700, England developed new trading links with the rest of the world: ✦ Portuguese and Spanish colonialists in the 1500s traded enslaved African people who were taken to the Americas and enslaved on plantations. England's involvement in this trade began in 1562. The trade of enslaved African people lasted for centuries and became the largest forced migration in history. ✦ In 1600, Elizabeth I issued a Charter to set up the East India Company to develop trade links with Asia. England developed links especially with India and traded cotton, silk, dyes and spices. ✦ As England's sea power grew under the Tudors, privateering increased. ✦ In 1660, Charles II issued a Charter to set up the Royal African Company, to manage the trade of enslaved African people as well as gold and silver.

1.2 Reasons for migration and patterns of settlement

Different groups of migrants were attracted to England during the years c.1500 to c.1700 because of attitudes towards religion, government and the developments in trade and the economy.

Protestant migrants

✚ Huguenots migrated from France in the 1500s and were welcomed by the Protestant King Edward VI.
✚ More Huguenots arrived after the St Bartholomew's Day Massacre in 1572.
✚ The greatest number of Huguenots migrated between 1670 and 1710, especially after it became illegal for French people to be Protestants in 1685.
✚ In 1681, King Charles II offered them denizen status.
✚ In 1709, the government passed the Foreign Protestant Naturalisation Act, allowing European Protestants to live in England providing they swore loyalty to the Crown.
✚ Before c1700, Palatines and German Protestants migrated to England for the opportunity of land and a better life. In 1709, approximately 13,000 Palatines migrated to England and settled at a refugee camp on Blackheath.

> **Key terms**
>
> **Privateering** When a ship attacks and steals from another ship at sea with the consent of a monarch or government
>
> **Charter** Written permission from the monarch giving rights and privileges to individuals and groups

Check your understanding and progress at **www.hoddereducation.co.uk/myrevisionnotes**

Jewish people

+ By the 1650s, the persecution of Jewish people in Europe was increasing. Cromwell agreed that they should be welcomed back into England after meeting with Rabbi Menasseh Ben Israel.
+ In 1656, a small group of Jewish migrants settled outside London, in Aldgate. They worshipped privately until a synagogue was built in Aldgate at the end of 1656. Over time, more Jewish people migrated and settled in trading ports including London, Liverpool and Portsmouth.

Indian people

+ Between the years c.1500 and c.1700, the East India Company set up trading posts all over India.
+ Some Indian people migrated to England to continue their work, for example looking after their employers' children (ayahs) or as servants.
+ Some men worked as lascars and stayed in England to work on ships. Some women migrated because they had married Englishmen.

African people

+ Between the years c.1500 and c.1700, African people were working in the royal court and in ordinary households (although black people have lived in England since the Roman Empire). They carried out a range of skilled jobs and were paid the same wages as other workers. The institution of slavery was not legal in England at the time (although there is evidence that enslavement did happen).
+ Some African people migrated to England because they were bought from, or escaped from, Portuguese traders. Some also migrated from Spain because of religious differences. They lived and worked in England as musicians, sailors and interpreters.

Key factors

Religion Religion attracted migrants to England in the years c.1500 to c.1700. England was a place of safety for Protestants from Catholic countries in Europe, especially France.

Organising knowledge

Use the information on pages 12–13 to complete the table below detailing examples of why different groups migrated to England in the years c.1500 to c.1700.

The role of religion	The role of the government	The role of global trade

The comparison question

Look at the exam-style question below and the two answers. Which answer is better for comparing the reasons for migration? Why?

Explain one way in which the reasons for migration to England in the years c.800 to c.1500 were different to the reasons for migration to England in the years c.1500 to c.1700. (4 marks)

Answer 1

People migrated to England in the years c.800 to c.1500 because they were invited by the king. However, people migrated to England in the years c.1500 to c.1700 because they needed a place of religious safety.

Answer 2

People migrated to England in the years c.800 to c.1500 because they were invited by the king. This included Jewish people, who migrated to England in 1070 because their moneylending skills were required by King William I. However, people migrated to England in the years c.1500 to c.1700 because they needed a place of religious safety. This included Protestant Huguenots from France, a Catholic country, who needed to escape religious persecution.

Key terms

St Bartholomew's Day Massacre When King Charles IX of France ordered the killing of Huguenot leaders in Paris. It is estimated that 3000 Huguenots were killed in Paris and 70,000 in the rest of France

Denizenship The process of denization was for an individual wealthy migrant (denizen) to be given the rights of English-born subjects in return for swearing exclusive loyalty to the English monarch

Rabbi A Jewish religious leader

Key migrant groups

Huguenots French Protestants

Palatines German Protestants. Most were poor farmers and their families

Lascar An Indian sailor who worked on the ships of the East India Company

Ayah A nursemaid or nanny employed by European people in India

2 The experience and impact of migrants

England became more prosperous between c.1500 and c.1700 because of the contribution of migrant communities. Migrants helped to develop religious tolerance, language and art.

2.1 The experience of migrants in England

REVISED ○

Protestants

+ Most Huguenots were successful in England. They found work with friends and relatives in industries including spinning, weaving and finance. Others began their own businesses.
+ However, most German Palatines struggled. Initially, people raised money to help the migrants, but this soon ran out. The Palatines did not have many skills and could not find labouring work. English people became hostile, fearing the Palatines would take jobs away. The government responded in 1709 by settling 3000 Palatines in Ireland.

Jewish people

+ As the Jewish migrant community in London increased, a larger synagogue was built in 1701 with permission from the authorities. Some Jewish people experienced success as merchants, bankers and doctors.
+ Jewish migrant communities in the seaports found work as tailors, shopkeepers and pawnbrokers. However, other Jewish migrants struggled financially and needed to rely on support such as donations of food, money and clothing.
+ Though more people accepted Jewish migrants, there is evidence of antisemitism, as Jewish people were forbidden to attend university, become lawyers or serve in the army. Pamphlets and songs also portrayed Jewish people as thieves and beggars.

African people

+ Some African migrants worked in England as weavers, servants and sailors.
+ By 1650, English merchants were involved in the trade of enslaved African people, and this led to racist treatment of some black people. In the late 1600s, it became fashionable for wealthy white people to have a black person as a servant, especially a child. Newspaper adverts offering rewards for runaways provide us with evidence that some African servants were unhappy.

Indian people

+ Some Indian sailors (lascars) settled in port cities including London, Liverpool, Glasgow and Cardiff. Some continued to work as sailors on ships or as labourers. Some Indian servants who returned with their masters were treated with respect and looked after, while others were replaced by English servants. Indian children were also used as servants and seen as status symbols to show their employers' wealth.

> **Key terms**
>
> **Printing press** A device invented in 1440 by Johannes Gutenberg to print pages using moveable type. Prior to this, books were written by monks in Latin
>
> **Brocade** A heavy silk fabric that is richly decorated using gold and silver thread

> **Revision task**
>
> Create a timeline detailing the experiences of migrants in England in the years c.1500 to c.1700. You could create a key and colour code the experiences of each migrant group. Mark any turning points (big changes) in their experiences.

> **Exam tip**
>
> Make sure you can support any arguments about the ways in which migrants impacted on early modern England with specific examples.

Check your understanding and progress at **www.hoddereducation.co.uk/myrevisionnotes**

2.2 The impact of migrants in England

Culture	✦ The migration of Huguenots and the building of their own churches led to more acceptance of religious difference in England.
	✦ In 1500, the five printers in England using the printing press were all European. Printing books led to new ideas being shared.
	✦ The Huguenots brought new words including 'brocade'. Road names in London also changed to reflect their skills, such as Petticoat Lane.
	✦ As Jewish communities spread, words such as 'synagogue' and 'rabbi' became as familiar as they had been in the twelfth century.
	✦ Some migrants became famous for their contributions to art and literature:
	  ✦ Hans Holbein, from Germany, famously painted portraits of King Henry VIII.
	  ✦ Polydore Vergil, from Italy, wrote books about English history.

Trade	✦ The cloth trade benefited from the skills of the Huguenots. England's silk production increased and was exported. English weavers learned techniques from the Huguenots. ✦ European migrants in England worked in the book trade and helped this trade to grow.
Industry	✦ The Huguenots brought new fabrics to English fashion, such as silk. They also helped to develop the steel industry in Sheffield. The Huguenots started the English paper industry. There were 200 paper mills in England by 1714. ✦ The Huguenots invested in the Bank of England in the seventeenth century. London became a major financial centre. ✦ Jewish migrants contributed to the English economy as merchants and financiers. Successful Jewish businessmen financially supported monarchs and noblemen.
Agriculture	✦ Dutch migrants changed the landscape of England by straightening rivers and building embankments, windmills and pumps. ✦ These changes to the Fens landscape led to changes in farming, including the introduction of geese and the planting of hemp.

Organising knowledge

Use the information on page 14 to complete the table below to categorise the experience of migrants in early modern England between c.1500 and c.1700.

	Relations with the authorities	Relations with the existing population
Protestants		
Jewish people		
African people		.
Indian people		

Organising knowledge

Use the information on pages 14–15 to complete the table below to show the change and continuity in the impact of migrants in England in the years c.1500 to c.1700.

The impact of migrants in early modern England	
Change **New ways that migrants impacted on England**	**Continuity** **Continued ways that migrants impacted on England**

3 Case studies

3.1 Sandwich and Canterbury in the sixteenth centuries

REVISED

The Flemish and Walloon migrant communities in Sandwich and Canterbury had very different experiences.

The Flemish community in Sandwich	The Walloon community in Canterbury
Flemish weavers were invited to Sandwich, with the permission of Elizabeth I's council, to help improve the economy by introducing a new skill and new business.	In 1575, the first Walloon community settled in Canterbury. Some were from Sandwich. Canterbury was experiencing a decline in visitors and trade, following the Reformation and the end of pilgrimages to the city. Elizabeth I's council gave permission to Canterbury to invite Walloon migrants to fill 100 empty houses.
In 1561, 400 Flemish migrants settled in Sandwich. More followed. The wealthy weavers made a lot of money for the town. By 1582, over half of the population of Sandwich were Flemish migrants. The weavers were given St Peter's Church for worship. They introduced new crops, including celery and carrots, to England.	Around 750 Walloon migrants filled these houses. They were allowed to use the Blackfriars monastery as a church, school and weavers' market for the production and sale of their goods.
However, because of fears of job-taking from the local community, restrictions were put in place on the Flemish migrants: ✦ 1569 – Only allowed to work as bricklayers, masons and carpenters if Englishmen had refused the work. They were banned from making shoes. ✦ 1581 – Towns ordered that migrants were only allowed to work in the cloth or fishing trades, and faced being fined if these laws were broken. ✦ 1582 – After an appeal by Flemish migrants, it was agreed by Elizabeth I's council that migrants could only work in cloth and trade. They were given permission to find work elsewhere and were protected from being fined.	The Walloons' success created jobs and increased trade. In addition, they developed new trades including silk dyeing, refining sugar and diamond cutting. There was less rivalry over jobs because these trades were new. The Walloon community had a group of 12 'elders' who worked with the local authorities to set rules, leading to better relations. By 1585 the local community started to fear there were too many migrants. New arrivals had to prove to the elders that they had migrated due to religious persecution and that their business would not compete with those of existing businesses in Canterbury.
Eventually, many Flemish migrant families left Sandwich and settled elsewhere.	In 1588, the Walloon migrants helped to prepare the city's defences against a Spanish invasion.

3.2 The experience of Huguenots in seventeenth-century England

REVISED

A second wave of Huguenot migration to England took place during the seventeenth century. King William III supported their migration because he wanted to strengthen the Protestant population in England, and wanted to use the skills of the Huguenots to make England prosperous.

During the second wave of Huguenot migration, half of the arrivals settled in London. Two important communities emerged in Soho and Spitalfields. Many of the Huguenots pursued businesses in skilled crafts such as textile weaving and watchmaking, and in professions such as law and banking. Some Huguenots arrived with nothing, after escaping persecution. A relief committee was set up and money was raised, including from King William and Queen Mary, to help these Huguenots. Some Huguenots settled in Soho, close to an existing community and a Huguenot church. Huguenots who settled in Spitalfields were given permission to build their own church, and by 1700 there were nine. These

> **Revision task**
>
> Consider the experiences of the migrant groups on this page. Create a table detailing how they were treated by the authorities (monarchs, town councils, guilds) and ordinary people.

churches allowed the Huguenots to keep their own identity but also enabled them to settle successfully because the local community could see that they were respectable, hardworking and offering support to the poor.

The Huguenot migrants were largely welcomed in London, where there was an anti-Catholic feeling, although there was some tension as some local people complained that the Huguenots were taking work. However, as migrants shared their skills and success with the English weavers, these tensions disappeared.

The Huguenots had a large impact on seventeenth century England:
+ Many of the Huguenots shared their success in silk weaving, and as gold and silversmiths.
+ Workshops produced a variety of silks including taffetas, brocades, and velvets.
+ Spitalfields was nicknamed 'weaver town', where large workshops were built, and the industry was very successful.
+ Some highly skilled Huguenots were admitted to the Weavers' Company, the guild that controlled weaving in the City of London.
+ Many of the Huguenots had been successful in business and finance, and they shared their experience and wealth by investing in the newly established Bank of England.
+ Some Huguenots participated in the increase in scientific experimentation and knowledge of the period and were invited to join the Royal Society (founded in 1660).

> ### Key term
> **Guild** An association of merchants or craftspeople who controlled membership and the quality of work produced across different trades

> ### Key groups
> **Flemish weavers in Sandwich** A group of Dutch Protestants invited to the town in the sixteenth century
>
> **Walloons** French-speaking Protestants from the Spanish Netherlands (today Belgium and the Netherlands) who fled persecution from the Catholic Spanish rulers

Eliminate irrelevance

Here is an exam-style question:

> Explain why there was an increase in migration to England in the years 1500 to 1700. (12 marks)

> You may use the following in your answer:
> + Flemish migrants in Sandwich
> + Huguenots
>
> You **must** also use information of your own.

Below is a paragraph which is part of an answer to the question above. Some parts of the answer are not relevant to the question. Identify these and draw a line through the information that is irrelevant, justifying your deletions in the margin.

There was an increase in migration to England in the years 1500 to 1700 because of the attraction of new opportunities for work and trade. In the sixteenth century, the authorities of Sandwich invited Flemish migrants to the town to introduce new skills and trade to the community. Sandwich had been a port town, but it fell into decline in the sixteenth century. The Flemish Protestants were invited to Sandwich with the hope that they would share their weaving skills and increase the success, wealth and prosperity of the town. In 1561, 25 Flemish households arrived in Sandwich. They built their own homes and were given St Peter's Church for worship. They introduced new crops, including celery and carrots, to England. The experience of the Flemish weavers began to change when the local community became worried that they were taking jobs from the people in the town. By 1581, the Flemish migrants were only allowed to work in the cloth or fishing trades. Many Flemish migrant families left Sandwich in 1582 and settled elsewhere in England. This led to an increase in migration to England in the years 1500 to 1700 because the success of the Flemish migrants, who settled with the permission of Queen Elizabeth I, encouraged more Flemish Protestant weavers to migrate and settle in England. They often settled in towns, like Sandwich, where there was already an existing migrant community with similar beliefs, language and culture.

Key topic 3: c.1700–c.1900: Migration in eighteenth- and nineteenth-century Britain

1 The context for migration

1.1 The changing context of British society

REVISED ●

The years c.1700 to c.1900 saw great changes in Britain which had an impact on migration.

Changes in government Migrant groups were attracted to Britain because it offered greater civil liberties and political freedom.	✛ Throughout the eighteenth century, only five per cent of the population of Britain could vote. The 1832 Reform Act gave the right to vote to more men. This was extended in 1867 and 1884 to working-class men. ✛ The Catholic Emancipation Act in 1829 allowed Catholics almost all the civil rights of Protestants. ✛ The restrictions on Jewish people (see page 14) were lifted in the 1830s	and they were able to become MPs from 1858. ✛ In 1807, Britain's slave trade was abolished. In 1833 slavery in the British Empire was forbidden. However, the enslaved African people were tied to the plantations as apprentices. Those who had become free, and could afford to migrate, were attracted to Britain.
Changes in industry Migrant groups were attracted to the greater job opportunities. The factories and docks needed workers.	✛ Between 1750 and 1850, there was an **Industrial Revolution** in Britain. Factories were built to meet the demand for manufactured goods, and workers were needed. Machines were built to increase the production of goods. Coal was mined to power factories.	✛ By the mid-nineteenth century, large industrial towns included Glasgow, Birmingham and Manchester. The population of towns grew from 5 million in 1700 to 32.5 million in 1900. Docks were built in Liverpool, London, Cardiff, Bristol and Glasgow.
Changes in transport Migrant groups could travel to and around Britain much more easily. Improved transport also provided job opportunities.	✛ Transport changed as, increasingly, raw materials were moved to factories and manufactured goods moved to markets. ✛ By 1820, there was a canal network that linked industrial towns and Britain's ports. ✛ The Liverpool to Manchester railway opened in 1830, making the transport of goods faster and cheaper. By 1900, five major railway companies operated across Britain.	✛ By 1840, there was a network of roads from London to all major cities. ✛ Steam power transformed shipping, connecting Britain to ports around the world. Ships sailed from Bristol and Liverpool to New York and Australia.
Growth of the British Empire Britain's contact with the world grew, leading to an increase in migration. The transatlantic slave trade led to an increase in forced migration.	✛ By 1900, Britain ruled one-fifth of the world's land and a quarter of the world's population. ✛ Britain used the countries in its Empire to sell its manufactured goods. Food and raw materials were exported from these countries too, which led to the decline of some local industries. ✛ Sugar from the **plantations** in British-owned West Indies (the Caribbean) made	merchants in port towns very wealthy. This was made possible because of the transatlantic slave trade and slave labour in colonies such as Barbados. ✛ In 1858, the British Government took over the control of India from the East India Company. ✛ In 1885, European powers began to colonise African countries. Britain controlled land in Southern Africa, Egypt and Sudan.

1.2 Reasons for migration and patterns of settlement

REVISED ●

Industrialisation led to people migrating from rural areas to towns. Different groups of migrants continued to be attracted to Britain. Some migrated voluntarily though many others were forced.

Irish migrants

✛ In the eighteenth century, Irish people came to Britain for seasonal work and then returned to Ireland. However, in the nineteenth century Irish

> **Key terms**
>
> **Industrial Revolution** A period when Britain changed from relying on farming and agriculture to focusing on manufacturing and factories

Check your understanding and progress at **www.hoddereducation.co.uk/myrevisionnotes**

people migrated because of high rents, poor land, a shortage of food and lack of jobs for Catholics in Ireland. Following the Great Famine of 1845, 2 million migrated to England, settling in London, Liverpool and Glasgow

European migrants

+ In the eighteenth century, aristocrats and clergy migrated from France, due to the French Revolution, to Britain because of its political stability.
+ In the nineteenth century, Germans were attracted by the freedom to think and express their political thoughts, as well as Britain's economic strength.
+ Italians were attracted by the opportunity to continue working in agriculture.

African migrants

+ By 1750, Britain was the largest participant in the transatlantic slave trade. This period of the trade and enslavement led to the forced migration of some African people to Britain and affected the lives of free black African people already living in Britain.

Asian migrants

+ After Britain took control of India in 1858, Britain's presence and trade increased. This led to thousands more Indian people migrating to Britain.
+ After being forced out of their land by the British government, some Indian princes migrated to Britain with their riches.
+ Some Indian students migrated to attend British universities.
+ Some Indian servants migrated to continue to work for the families who had colonised their land.
+ Some lascars worked on the ships of the East India Company, eventually settling in Britain.
+ Following an increase in trade with China, there was a demand for Chinese lascars in Britain.

Jewish migrants

+ As restrictions on Jewish people were lifted (see page 14), Britain became more attractive to Jewish migrants.
+ Jewish refugees fleeing persecution in the Russian Empire migrated to Britain because of its already established Jewish communities, and because it appeared to be a place of safety.

Key terms

Plantation An estate on which crops, such as sugar, were grown

Great Famine A famine that occurred in Ireland in 1845–49 when the potato crop failed

French Revolution A period of major social upheaval between 1789 and 1799 when the monarchy was replaced by a republic

Refugee A person who has been forced to leave their country due to war, persecution or natural disaster

Russian Empire Lands in Asia and eastern Europe ruled over by the Tsarist regime between 1721 and 1917

Key factors

Economic influences Migrants were attracted to Britain during the years c.1700 to c.1900 because of the employment opportunities provided by the Industrial Revolution and the expansion of the British Empire.

Analysing factors

You need to understand the role that factors had on the reasons for migration to Britain and patterns of settlement. Rank order the factors below that explain the reason for migration to Britain and patterns of settlement in the years c.1700 to c.1900, beginning with the **most** important. Explain your decisions by adding more details to each factor.

For a reminder about each factor see page 5.
+ Government
+ Church
+ Religion
+ Economic influences
+ Attitudes in society

Organising knowledge

Use the information on pages 18–19 to complete the table below to show the change and continuity in the reasons for migration to Britain in the years c.1700 to c.1900.

Reasons for migration in eighteenth- and nineteenth-century Britain	
Change	**Continuity**
New reasons for migration	**Same reasons for migration**

2 The experience and impact of migrants

2.1 Relations with the authorities, the existing population and the role of the media

Most migrants faced prejudice from the existing British society and the media. This tended to continue when there was competition for jobs and when migrant cultures were visibly different. Some migrant groups became integrated into their new communities.

Irish migrants

✦ Irish migrants took on labouring work in docks, mines and railways. The work carried out by Irish navvies was dangerous and many were killed or injured.

✦ Irish migrants faced prejudice and hostility for several reasons, including competition for jobs, their Catholicism, and a feeling that the English were superior due to their Anglo-Saxon heritage.

Jewish migrants

✦ Most Jewish migrants settled in London.

✦ Existing Jewish communities were worried about how the arrival of thousands of poor Jewish migrants would affect their relationship with the authorities and the existing population.

✦ New Jewish migrants were urged by the authorities to learn English and assimilate alongside keeping their traditions.

✦ The increase in Jewish migrants led to overcrowding and competition for jobs. This, in turn, led to resentment, which was increased by the media.

✦ However, in 1858, Jewish people were able to become Members of Parliament. In 1871, they were able to take up fellowships at Oxford and Cambridge Universities.

European migrants

✦ European migrants had positive experiences in Britain as they set up small businesses that were successful. These included butcher's shops, brewers, bakeries and restaurants. Italian migrants set up businesses selling ice cream, and some worked as street musicians. They set up schools, hospitals, newspapers and shops.

✦ Some European migrants experienced hostility when they settled in areas of cities such as London.

African migrants

✦ There were 10,000 black African people living in Britain by the mid-eighteenth century. Their legal status was unclear. A legal case (1772) stated that slavery did not exist in Britain, rather than stating that slavery existed and was illegal.

✦ Some African people could not find work in Britain and relied on begging. In 1786, the 'Committee for the Relief of the Black Poor' was set up to organise the exodus of African people to West Africa and establish Sierra Leone.

✦ In the nineteenth century, the population of black people began to grow in British cities including London, Liverpool, Glasgow and Cardiff.

Asian migrants

✦ Some ayahs arrived in Britain with a return ticket. However, some were left stranded without employment or accommodation.

✦ In the mid-nineteenth century, a group of English women set up a hostel for abandoned ayahs that was later run by a Christian organisation, the London City Mission. They would try to find the ayahs work or a ticket back to India.

Key terms

Navvies Manual labourers from Ireland who dug canals and built railways

Assimilate Become similar to

Revision task

Create a timeline of the experiences and impact of migrants in Britain in the years c.1700 to c.1900. Draw your line down the middle of the page. Record experiences on one side of the line and impact on the other side of the line. You could use different colours for the different migrant groups.

Check your understanding and progress at **www.hoddereducation.co.uk/myrevisionnotes**

- Shipping companies were responsible for Chinese lascars while they were in Britain, and for their return home.
- Some lascars chose to stay and found work in ports such as Liverpool. Those who could not find work turned to begging or stealing.
- Chinese migrants were viewed negatively by the existing population and the media and barred from some jobs.
- Hostels, such as The Strangers Home in London, were opened to help lascars who struggled to find work.

2.2 The impact of migrants in Britain

Culture	- Improved transport enabled newspapers to be distributed quickly and widely. A German migrant, Paul Reuter, set up the Reuter's News Agency in 1851 and was the first to report accurate stories of international importance. - A Russian Jewish man, Michael Marks, migrated to Britain in the nineteenth century to escape persecution. In 1894, he was joined by Tom Spencer. They opened Marks and Spencer stores throughout Britain. - The first Indian restaurant in London was opened by Sake Dean Mahomed.
Trade	- The canals and railways built by Irish and Italian navvies enabled the movement of raw materials and finished goods more easily.
Industry	- Many migrant companies were successful and helped the British economy. For example, Johann Jacob Schweppe was a German-Swiss migrant who developed carbonated water. - Migrant businesses were successful because of the financial investment from German bankers in the City of London, including the Rothschilds. - Italian migrants popularised ice cream.
Politics	- In 1787, the Society for the Abolition of the Slave Trade was formed to educate the British public about the horrors of the trade through meetings, published books and pamphlets. Black African people in Britain, such as Olaudah Equiano and Ottobah Cugoano, were an important part of this movement and shared their experiences. In 1807, the slave trade was abolished, and, in 1833, so was slavery in the British Empire. - The Chartist movement emerged in the nineteenth century to convince Parliament to give working-class men the vote. Two leading Chartists were migrants; Feargus O'Connor, Irish-born, and William Cuffay, whose father had been enslaved in the Caribbean. - Karl Marx and Friedrich Engels migrated because of the freedom Britain offered to develop their ideas. Marx and Engels wrote *Manifesto of the Communist Party* in which they urged the working classes to unite and challenge the political system.
The urban environment	- Canals and railways were built throughout Britain by Irish and Italian navvies, including the Leeds to Liverpool canal. - Improved transport helped industrial towns to grow quickly. Migrants settled in all parts of Britain.

Identify the view

Read the exam-style question below and identify the view that is offered about the impact of migrants in the years c.1700 to c.1900.

> 'The impact on culture was the most significant consequence of migration to Britain in the years c.1700 to c.1900.' How far do you agree? Explain your answer. (16 marks, with a further 4 marks available for spelling, punctuation and grammar.)

1 What view is offered by the statement about the impact of migrants in Britain in the years c.1700 to c.1900?

_____

_____

2 How far do you agree? Use your knowledge to agree and disagree with the statement given in the question. To plan an answer to this question, copy and complete the following table.

Knowledge which agrees with the statement	
Knowledge which disagrees with the statement	

3 Now write paragraphs that agree and disagree with the statement:

The statement is partially correct …

The statement is partially incorrect …

3. Case studies

3.1 Liverpool in the nineteenth century

By the end of the nineteenth century, Liverpool was the second most profitable port in the world (after London).

+ Liverpool made huge profits from the transatlantic slave trade until the abolition of the trade in 1807.
+ Liverpool was a centre of trade with America, for example with cotton picked by enslaved African people, which was imported to Britain from the plantations, then exported to factories in cities.

Liverpool's trading links and job opportunities made it attractive to migrants.

Irish migrants	+ Irish migrants settled in Liverpool because of the job opportunities at the docks and on ships. + Many male migrants found employment in poorly paid manual labour jobs that involved long hours and hard conditions. They eventually dominated jobs at the docks. + Many female migrants found work as maids. + Some Irish migrants set up successful businesses in Liverpool and participated in local politics. + As the Irish community grew in Liverpool, separate social areas appeared, including Irish pubs and businesses. + Irish migrants were often blamed for crime in the city. + The 'Scouse' accent originates from Irish speakers.
Indian migrants	+ It was common to see Indian sailors in Liverpool throughout the nineteenth century. + Some also worked as street sweepers or set up lodging houses for other sailors. + Many Indians who migrated to Liverpool married British women.
African sailors	+ As trade with Africa increased, African sailors also migrated to Liverpool. + African sailors worked in hard conditions for lower pay.
Chinese migrants	+ From the 1850s, Chinese seamen migrated to Liverpool as silk, cotton and tea were imported from China. + In the late nineteenth century, Chinese shops and cafés increased in the city. + Liverpool has the most established 'Chinatown' in Europe.

3.2 The experience of Jewish migrants in the East End of London in the late nineteenth century

Jewish migrants in the late nineteenth century settled in Whitechapel (and Spitalfields), in London's East End, as Jewish communities were already established there. The existing Jewish community worked hard to support the new migrants. The London Jewish Free School opened in 1822 and was important in helping integration while maintaining cultural and religious traditions. The Jewish Lads' Brigade was founded in 1895 with the aim of instilling British values in Jewish boys. The Russian Vapour Baths stood opposite the synagogue in Brick Lane in the East End. It was owned by a leader of the Jewish community, Benjamin Schewzik, and enabled Russian Jewish men to bathe before the Sabbath.

However, rising poverty and unemployment led to antisemitic hostility and attacks by the non-Jewish population towards the increasing numbers of Jewish migrants in Whitechapel:

+ Many English people believed Jewish people were taking their jobs.
+ Jewish people worked in illegal sweatshops for long hours and little pay despite trade unions' efforts to improve working conditions. This led to Jewish sweatshop owners being able to produce goods more cheaply than factories could.
+ Communication was difficult because some Jewish people only spoke Yiddish rather than English.

Key terms

Chinatown A part of a town or port where the population is mostly of Chinese heritage

Sweatshop A place where cheap clothes are made, often with workers forced to work in terrible conditions

Inquest A legal investigation into an incident, e.g. a death

Key group

Irish navvies Many of the new docks in Liverpool were built by the Irish navviess

Organising knowledge

Use the information on page 22 to complete the table below for the migrant groups in Liverpool and the East End of London during eighteenth- and nineteenth-century Britain.

	Migrants in Liverpool	Jewish migrants in the East End of London
Reasons for migration		
Experiences of migrants		
Impact of migrants		

Exam tip

When you revise the experiences of migrants in Liverpool and the East End of London, consider evidence that shows they had positive **and** negative experiences.

The comparison question

Look at the exam-style question below and the two answers. Which answer is better for comparing the experiences of the migrant groups? Why?

> Explain one way in which the experiences of Walloon migrants in Canterbury in the sixteenth century were different to the experiences of Jewish migrants in the East End of London in the nineteenth century. (4 marks)

Answer 1

The Walloon migrants in Canterbury in the sixteenth century were welcomed by the existing population because they used their skills of spinning and weaving fine cloth and silk to increase trade. This created jobs for those people already living in Canterbury. However, the Jewish migrants in the East End of London in the nineteenth century experienced hostility from the existing population who believed they were trying to take their jobs. Jewish migrants worked in illegal sweatshops for longer hours and less pay, leading to the creation of cheaper goods than those made in local factories.

Answer 2

The Walloon migrants in Canterbury in the sixteenth century were welcomed by the existing population because they created jobs. However, the Jewish migrants in the East End of London in the nineteenth century experienced hostility from the existing population who believed they were trying to take their jobs.

My Revision Notes: Pearson Edexcel GCSE (9-1) Migrants in Britain

Key topic 4: c.1900–present: Migration in modern Britain

1 The context for migration

1.1 The changing context of British society

REVISED ●

The years c.1900 to the present day also saw great changes in Britain that continued to have an impact on migration.

Changes in government Migrant groups were attracted to Britain because it offered greater political representation, legal protection and employment opportunities. British law gave support to asylum seekers.	After 1900, laws were passed that made Parliament more representative and that changed people's lives. The NHS, introduced in 1948, gave people free healthcare and was paid for by taxation. Laws were passed regarding immigration and nationality including the 1905 **Aliens Act**, and the 1948 **British Nationality Act**. Britain joined the European Economic Community (EEC) in 1973. The Maastricht Treaty, signed in 1992, created the **European Union (EU)** and increased the movement of people between Europe and Britain. Britain voted to leave the EU in 2016.
Changes in the economy Migrant groups were attracted to Britain because it offered employment opportunities.	British cities and factories needed to be rebuilt after the Second World War. Developments in aeroplanes and ships allowed for the faster and easier movement of people and goods. British industry, for example coal mining, faced cheaper competition from companies overseas.
Changes in the British Empire Migrant groups were attracted to Britain because of previous connections.	Soldiers from countries in the British Empire fought alongside Britain in the First and Second World Wars. The twentieth century saw the end of the British Empire as British colonies gained independence. This process is known as 'decolonisation'. As the British Empire ended, the Commonwealth emerged. This was an independent association of countries that had once been part of the British Empire.

1.2 Reasons for migration and patterns of settlement

REVISED ●

Although migrants from other countries had always been in Britain, the events of the twentieth century, including two world wars, saw more mass migration into Britain than ever before.

Irish migrants

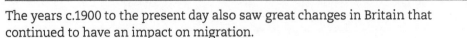

+ As with migrants from other countries, Irish people migrated to Britain after the Second World War for jobs rebuilding houses and factories, and in the transport system and the NHS.

European migrants

+ Over 250,000 Belgians migrated to Britain for safety when Germany invaded Belgium in 1914.
+ Workers from Europe also migrated after the Second World War to help rebuild Britain and to work in the NHS.
+ After Britain joined the EEC in 1973, the 1988 Immigration Act ensured that economic migrants from within the EEC could enter and remain in Britain for work. The Maastricht Treaty introduced EU citizenship for all nationals of member states, not just workers. This continued while Britain remained a member of the EU until 2016.

> **Key terms**
>
> **NHS** The National Health Service was set up in 1948 to provide free healthcare in Britain. At the time this included doctors, hospitals and dentists
>
> **Aliens Act** This allowed only those individuals with jobs or money to migrate and was the first Act that restricted who could migrate to Britain.

Migrants from the British Empire and the Commonwealth

+ During the First and Second World Wars, men from countries colonised by the British Empire fought in the British Army. During both wars, migrants from the colonies, including the Caribbean and Africa, moved to Britain to work for the war effort.
+ People from the Caribbean migrated to help rebuild Britain after the Second World War. Those who migrated between 1948 and 1973 are known as the 'Windrush generation' after the first ship that brought migrants from the Caribbean to Britain.
+ After India gained independence and partition followed, many Asian people migrated to Britain for safety.
+ Indian people were forced to leave Kenya (1967) and Uganda (1972). Those with British passports fled to Britain for safety.

Refugees and asylum seekers

+ The British government accepted well-qualified Jewish refugees from Nazi Germany in the 1930s as it became clear that they were being persecuted. The British government then decided to help Jewish children rather than any more Jewish adults, which led to the Kindertransport. This stopped in 1939 when war was declared, and the borders were closed.
+ European refugees from the Second World War migrated to Britain to stay safe, including refugees from Communist regimes in Eastern Europe such as Poland.
+ In 1951, Britain signed up to the United Nations Convention on Refugees, promising to offer asylum to refugees facing persecution. The number of refugees who applied to Britain for asylum increased throughout the late twentieth century and have included people from Somalia, Afghanistan and Ukraine.

Key group

Refugee Someone who is forced to leave their country to find safety from persecution and/or conflict

Asylum seeker A refugee who is waiting to be legally accepted into a country

Complete the paragraph

Below are an exam-style question and a paragraph which is part of an answer to this question. The paragraph gives a reason but does not go on to support or develop the explanation.

1 Rewrite the paragraph with precise supporting knowledge and a full explanation linking back to the question.

2 Complete the answer to this question:

Explain why migration to Britain increased in the years c.1900 to the present day. (12 marks)

You may use the following in your answer:
+ EU membership
+ Refugees and asylum seekers

You **must** also use information of your own.

There was an increase in migration to Britain in the years c.1900 to the present day because people looked for safety after experiencing persecution in their own country.

Key terms

British Nationality Act People living in British colonies were given British citizenship, and passports, which gave them the right to enter Britain and stay for as long as they wanted. The 1948 Act was not intended to bring non-white subjects to Britain; it was hoped that white settler families in Canada, Australia, New Zealand and South Africa would be encouraged to return

European Union (EU) This was established by the Maastricht Treaty, signed in 1992, and allowed the freedom of movement of all EU citizens

Partition In 1947, India gained independence from Britain and was split into India and Pakistan

Kindertransport During the 1930s, the British government dropped visa and entry requirements to allow Jewish children to leave Nazi Germany immediately and migrate to Britain for safety

United Nations An international organisation that aims to achieve world peace

Asylum The protection given by a state to someone who has left their country due to fear of persecution

Revision task

Create a timeline of the key events in British society from c.1900 to the present day. For each event, explain how it attracted migrants to Britain.

2 The experience and impact of migrants

2.1 Relations with the authorities and existing population, and the role of the media

Anti-migrant attitudes among British society increased after 1900. Fears over job losses were blamed on migrants. Many local communities welcomed and supported migrants, but prejudice and racism became a part of everyday life for many. Political parties formed in the twentieth century to oppose immigration included the National Front in 1967 and the British National Party in 1982. The positive and negative attitudes towards migrants in Britain were encouraged by the media.

Irish migrants

+ Some experienced prejudice throughout this period. Irish nurses in the NHS experienced hostility and abuse.
+ However, some were also welcomed by the existing British population.

European migrants

+ Belgians were welcomed during the First World War, but the British government made it clear that they were only expected to stay for the duration of the war and in 1918 they were given a ticket home. The majority returned to Belgium.
+ The British Parliament passed the British Nationality and Status of Aliens Act (1914) making Germans enemy aliens. Some British people turned against them, and the media fuelled anti-German feeling, leading to an increase in violence towards Germans and their businesses. Some Germans were deported while others were interned until the end of the First World War.
+ Germans and Italians were interned again during the Second World War. However, British people did not support this action and so it soon ended.

Migrants from the British Empire and the Commonwealth

+ There was tension between the lascars and the existing population over competition for jobs. Riots broke out in cities such as Liverpool and Cardiff in 1919.
+ In 1968, Enoch Powell (Conservative MP for Wolverhampton, where there was a Caribbean and Asian migrant community) made his anti-migrant 'Rivers of Blood' speech against non-white migrants. Some British people marched in support.
+ Riots broke out in Brixton in 1981 following accusations of police brutality towards the children of Caribbean migrants. Young black men in Brixton experienced discrimination in jobs, housing and from the police.
+ Riots also occurred in other cities with high migrant populations, including Burnley in 2001.

Refugees and asylum seekers

+ Many Polish refugees did not want to return to a Poland controlled by the Soviet Union, a communist dictatorship.
+ The British Parliament passed the Polish Resettlement Act (1947) to allow Polish servicemen to remain with their families in Britain. Polish migrants found work, particularly in mining, were gradually accepted and formed communities in industrial towns.
+ After 1945, many Jewish child refugees were allowed to stay in Britain because their families had died in Nazi concentration camps.

Key terms

Intern To hold someone prisoner, mainly for political reasons

Commonwealth Immigrants Act (1962) This introduced a voucher system for migrants with a valuable skill or who could take a job where there was a shortage. This ended the automatic right for those with a Commonwealth passport to live and work in Britain. In 1968, the number of vouchers available were reduced so that only those born in Britain or with parents/grandparents born in Britain could apply

Race Relations Acts From 1965, it was illegal to discriminate against any person because of their race in public facilities. In 1968, this was extended to include discrimination in housing and employment. From 1976, it became illegal to discriminate on the grounds of race, nationality or ethnic origin in employment, education, training and housing. This did not apply to police though.

Immigration Act From 1971, vouchers were replaced with work permits for set periods of time, but this did not apply to migrants with British-born parents or grandparents

Revision task

Can you find examples of more first-generation migrants who have had an impact on Britain in the twentieth century? Add details to your revision notes.

Check your understanding and progress at **www.hoddereducation.co.uk/myrevisionnotes**

Equal rights movements were formed by migrants throughout the twentieth century. These included the League of Coloured Peoples in London and the West African Students' Union, formed to encourage an end to the British Empire and racism. Following the Race Relations Acts in 1965, 1968 and 1976 the experiences of migrants in Britain changed. Three acts were needed to extend the extent of discrimination covered each time. These laws were passed by Parliament to end the discrimination that migrant communities faced and to ensure they were treated equally to white people.

Exam tip

It is important that you can explain parliamentary legislation during this period. Link cause and consequence directly.

2.2 The impact of migrants in Britain

REVISED ○

Culture	✦ Migrants brought their religions to Britain. ✦ Festivals and celebrations of the migrant communities were brought to Britain, including the Hindu celebration of Diwali, the festival of lights. ✦ Migrants have brought new foods to Britain including the kebab introduced by Turkish Cypriots and Turks and Indian food, such as the curry. ✦ Migrants, and their descendants, have played a key part in sport, politics, music and the media. Individuals include Mo Farah (a gold medal-winning British athlete born in Somalia).
Politics	✦ As a result of increased migration to Britain, Parliament passed legislation including the Commonwealth Immigrants Acts with the aim of reducing migration to Britain, the Race Relations Acts which made discrimination illegal, and the Immigration Act, which further aimed to reduce migration to Britain. ✦ Pressure groups formed in response to a rise in migration to Britain. These included the National Front (1967) who wanted a ban on all non-white migration to Britain and the Anti-Nazi League (1977) who disrupted protests by racist groups. ✦ Other pressure groups have formed to raise awareness of discrimination and racism in Britain, including Show Racism the Red Card (SRTRC).
Urban environment	✦ Migrant communities regenerated the run-down and damaged areas of Britain's cities where they were forced to live. They introduced new businesses and rebuilt houses. ✦ Restaurants serving food from migrant communities, including Chinese and Indian cuisine, became common in towns and cities.
Public services	✦ Migrants from the Caribbean worked for London Transport as bus drivers, bus conductors and station staff. ✦ Migrant workers were vital to the NHS from its beginning in 1948. Nurses were recruited from the Caribbean. Many NHS doctors were Jewish or European refugees from Nazi-occupied Europe. ✦ By 2003, 29.4 per cent of NHS doctors and 43.5 per cent of NHS nurses were born outside of Britain.
Economy	✦ Migrant workers played an important role in rebuilding the British economy after two world wars.

Understand the chronology

The events of the twentieth century have led to change for migrants in Britain. Using pages 24–27, place the events listed below in the correct chronological sequence in the table. On a separate sheet of paper, explain how each event led to change for migrants in Britain.

A British Nationality Act

B Britain joined the EEC

C Britain signed up to the United Nations Convention on Refugees

D Aliens Act

E Race Relations Act

F Enoch Powell's 'Rivers of Blood' speech

G Riots in Brixton

H London Transport paid migrants' fares from the Caribbean

I National Front was formed

J Britain voted to leave the EU

Date	Event
1905	
1948	
1951	
1956	
1965	
1967	
1968	
1973	
1981	
2016	

3 Case studies

3.1 Bristol in the mid-twentieth century

After the 1948 British Nationality Act was passed, Caribbean migrants were attracted to British cities including Bristol for work and to help rebuild. Their experiences included:

+ difficulties finding homes because racist landlords refused to rent to black people
+ being forced to live in the St Paul's area because emptier, war-damaged houses were available there
+ prejudice, racism and violence from some of the existing population, who believed the migrants took jobs and housing from them
+ colour bars
+ discrimination such as a Bristol bus company banning the employment of 'coloured people'* as bus drivers or conductors. In 1963, the West Indian Development Council (WIDC) (see below) boycotted Bristol's buses until the colour bar was lifted. The Bristol Bus Boycott was a success and supported by people of many ethnicities. It made national news and the colour bar was lifted that year.
+ The Bristol West Indian Cricket Club was set up in 1964 for people from the Caribbean.
+ In 1966, the Bamboo Club opened, with music and a restaurant, to cater specifically for Bristol's Caribbean community. It was open to white and black Bristolians.

Migrants have had a large impact on Bristol society:

+ In 1962, the WIDC was formed by Owen Henry and Roy Hackett to support Caribbean migrants. They campaigned against racism and helped black people find better education, jobs and housing. In 1975, this became known as the West Indian Parents and Friends Association and is still active today.
+ Bristol became one of the first cities in Britain to have its own Race Equality Council working to improve education and housing for migrants.
+ The first St Paul's Festival took place in 1968. By 1979, this had become a platform for Caribbean and African artists to respond to events happening across the country. From 1991, it has been known as St Paul's Carnival.
+ In 2015, a series of murals were unveiled to celebrate black history in the city. They celebrate the 'seven saints of St Paul's' including Roy Hackett and Carmen Beckford (one of the founding members of the St Paul's Carnival).

> **Key term**
>
> **Colour bar** When people of colour are denied access to the same rights, opportunities and facilities as white people

> * 'Coloured people' was a phrase used to describe people with darker skin tones in the UK. This term is now derogatory.

3.2 The experience of Asian migrants in Leicester from 1945

+ Asian migrants were attracted to Leicester to work in the textiles and shoe industries. As they settled, the city and existing community attracted more migrants in the years that followed. By 1972, there were Hindu temples, Sikh gurdwaras, mosques, an Islamic foundation and Asian social and welfare clubs in Leicester.
+ Asian migrants in Leicester experienced hostility from the existing population. Colour bars were common. Asian migrants were forced to take on jobs that they were overqualified for and accept lower wages than their white colleagues. However, there were protests against colour bars and many people, of all ethnicities, fighting against racism, such as the Imperial Typewriters strike in 1974.
+ Following the expulsion of Asian people from Uganda in 1972, many were attracted to the existing migrant community in Leicester. Leicester City Council responded by placing an advertisement in the Ugandan newspapers to deter them from migrating to the city. Nevertheless, over a

> **Key factors**
>
> **Economic influences** Migrants in the twentieth century were attracted to Bristol and Leicester for employment opportunities.
>
> **Attitudes in society** The experiences of migrants in Bristol and Leicester were very much dependent on the positive and negative attitudes of society towards immigration and the migrant communities.

fifth of the Ugandan refugees arrived in Leicester and were helped to find homes and jobs by the British Asian Welfare Society and other charities. The National Front protested in Leicester with marches in 1974 and 1979.

Organising knowledge

Use the information on page 28 to complete the table below detailing the experiences of migrants in Bristol and Leicester in the years c.1900 to the present day.

	Relations with the authorities	Relations with the existing population
Migrants in Bristol		
Asian migrants in Leicester		

Exam tip

When writing about the experience of migrants in Bristol and Leicester, remember to include a range of experiences and consider their relations with the authorities and the existing population.

The comparison question

Look at the exam-style question below and the two answers. Which answer is better for comparing the experiences of the migrant groups? Why?

> Explain one way in which the experiences of Jewish migrants in the East End of London in the late nineteenth century were similar to the experiences of Asian migrants in Leicester from 1945. (4 marks)

Answer 1

Jewish migrants in the East End of London in the nineteenth century and Asian migrants in Leicester both experienced support from the existing population. BBC Radio Leicester broadcast an Asian programme in English for migrants in Leicester in 1976. This supported the Asian migrants ability to connect and integrate with the existing population.

Answer 2

Jewish migrants in the East End of London in the nineteenth century and Asian migrants in Leicester both experienced support from the existing population. The London Jewish Free School was opened by members of the Jewish community and was important in helping the migrants integrate while maintaining cultural and religious traditions. BBC Radio Leicester broadcast an Asian programme in English for migrants in Leicester. This supported the Asian migrant's ability to connect and integrate with the existing population.

Part 2: Notting Hill, c.1948–c.1970

1 The local context of Notting Hill

1.1 The reasons for Caribbean migration to the area

REVISED ●

People from the Caribbean migrated to Britain in the 1950s for work, which partly involved rebuilding Britain after the Second World War. Caribbean migrants settled in Notting Hill, London for a range of reasons:

✛ Notting Hill was close to Paddington station, where the train from the shipping port stopped. Officials from High Commissions of Caribbean countries, including Jamaica and Barbados, and volunteers would help newly arrived migrants find a place to stay.

✛ In the 1950s, many landlords were not willing to rent houses to black people. This behaviour was not illegal at the time. This left Caribbean migrants with little choice of where to live and they had to accept the neglected properties of the landlords in Notting Hill who would rent to them.

✛ The presence of some black people already living in Notting Hill led to other Caribbean migrants settling here. Caribbean migrants felt safer here after being made to feel unwelcome in other areas of London and Britain.

✛ As more Caribbean migrants settled in Notting Hill, the community grew to include market stalls and restaurants selling Caribbean food, making it more attractive.

> **Key term**
>
> **Houses of Multiple Occupation (HMOs)** Houses that are rented to many households, rather than to one family or one household

1.2 The problems of housing

REVISED ●

In the 1950s, houses in Notting Hill were neglected. Landlords solved the problem of struggling to rent these out by renting them to Caribbean migrants. The migrants were taken advantage of and charged rents that were higher than were charged to white tenants. Overcrowding was common.

Landlords applied to change their properties into Houses of Multiple Occupation (HMOs). This allowed more than one household in a house, with shared bathroom and/or kitchen facilities. The Caribbean migrants had no legal protection against these living conditions.

Peter Rachman was one of the few landlords in Notting Hill who would rent properties to Caribbean migrants. Rachman may have believed that he was helping the migrant community by renting homes to them, but the conditions of the properties were overcrowded, unhygienic and unpleasant. The authorities did not take action to stop the migrant community being treated in this way.

> **Key individuals**
>
> **Peter Rachman** A polish immigrant landlord in London. He had grown wealthy in the 1950s through crime. By 1959, he owned 80 properties in Notting Hill and was making a lot of money from their rent. He died in 1962, aged 43
>
> **Bruce Kenrick** Bruce Kenrick was a minister in the Church of Scotland, and later the United Reformed Church, who lived in Notting Hill from 1963

1.3 Bruce Kenrick and the Notting Hill Housing Trust

REVISED ●

Bruce Kenrick was shocked by the housing conditions and wanted to improve them. Kenrick raised £20,000 to buy a house to rent out to poor families. He was a Christian minister and supported by the Notting Hill Methodist Church. Following this success, in 1963 Kenrick set up the Notting Hill Housing Trust (NHHT) charity to raise money to help provide people with good quality affordable housing. Kenrick and the NHHT helped to improve the lives of migrants.

1.4 The development of Portobello Road market

Portobello Road is in the centre of Notting Hill. There has been a market on Portobello Road since the nineteenth century. From the 1950s, the market started to sell food and vegetables from the Caribbean, such as yams and sweet potatoes, for the growing community. Some Caribbean migrants started businesses selling Caribbean hot meals and snacks at the market. In the 1960s, a music scene developed on Portobello Road. Island Records, a Jamaican company, moved their base to a nearby street, Basing Street. Music shops and live venues followed that were welcomed by the community.

Memory map

Create a memory map detailing the living conditions in Notting Hill for Caribbean migrants. Add some key words from the information on pages 30–31 and your own knowledge to the diagram below. Use two different colours to show whether they are positive or negative for the migrants. To help you remember the information, you could add small drawings.

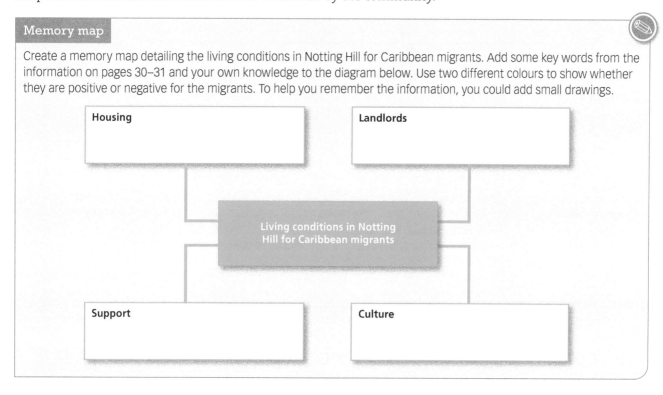

You're the examiner

Below is an exam-style question.

Describe two features of the development of Portobello Road market. (4 marks)

1   Below are a mark scheme and an answer to this question. Read them both and decide how many marks the answer would get. Write the mark along with a justification for your choice below.

Mark scheme

Award 1 mark for each valid feature identified up to a maximum of two features. The second mark should be awarded for supporting information.

From the 1950s, the Portobello Road market sold Caribbean food. This included yams and sweet potatoes.

Mark [ ]   Reason _____

_____

2   Now suggest what the student needs to do to achieve more marks.
3   Write an answer that would achieve more marks.

2 The influence of Caribbean cultures

As the Caribbean migrant community in Notting Hill grew, they developed their own identity. However, migrant-owned businesses experienced harassment from the police.

Shops and markets	<ul><li>Shops and market stalls sold foods from the Caribbean.</li><li>This included food flavoured with herbs and spices including thyme, fresh ginger and tabasco sauce.</li></ul>
Cafés and restaurants	<ul><li>There was a colour bar in Notting Hill in the 1950s and Caribbean migrants were prevented from entering many pubs, cafés and restaurants.</li><li>The first pub to serve black people in London opened on All Saints Road: The Apollo.</li><li>In 1959, Frank Crichlow opened the El Rio café. He served Caribbean food and it was popular with migrants and London celebrities.</li><li>Other pubs, cafés and restaurants owned by black people followed in the 1960s.</li></ul>
Nightclubs	<ul><li>The colour bar also operated in nightclubs and black people were refused entry.</li><li>In 1968, the Metro Club opened in Notting Hill. It was a youth club, community centre and nightclub for black people.</li><li>Members of the migrant community hosted shebeens in their homes or in abandoned buildings.</li><li>The police often raided the shebeens, explaining that people were selling alcohol without a licence, which was, and is, illegal.</li></ul>
Entertainment	<ul><li>Migrant houses would use radios to pick up foreign radio stations that played Motown, reggae and R&B (rhythm and blues).</li><li>Caribbean migrants seized the opportunity to open businesses that sold records by black artists because it was not available in London.</li><li>In the 1950s, people began listening to music via sound systems. They were used in houses and on the streets to play music performed by black artists.</li><li>In 1969, Basing Street studios opened. It was used by Bob Marley.</li></ul>

2.1 The development of All Saints Road

REVISED ⬤

Shops and restaurants owned by Caribbean migrants opened on All Saints Road, one of the main roads in Notting Hill. This road became filled with businesses owned by black migrants in the 1950s. One of these was the Mangrove Restaurant, owned by Frank Crichlow (see page 36). These shops and restaurants became targets of police harassment and racism. By the 1960s, All Saints Road had become a centre of black activism. The Black Panthers (see page 36) held meetings and the organisers of the Notting Hill carnival met here.

> **Key term**
>
> **Shebeens** Unofficial nightclubs with music, dancing and gambling

2.2 Mutual self-help organisations

REVISED ⬤

Black people in Notting Hill worked together. Organisations were set up so that the community could support one another. The London Free School was set up in 1966 to run classes for young people and offered support with childcare. The Black People's Information Centre was set up in 1970 to offer legal support and education on black history. Partner schemes were set up to help members of the migrant community buy their own home. These schemes had been used throughout the Caribbean and helped people to save to buy a house.

> **Revision task**
>
> Make your own copy of the table on this page. Add further examples of how Caribbean culture influenced Notting Hill.

Complete the answer

Below is an exam-style question and an answer. The answer identifies two features but does not develop them with any supporting knowledge. Annotate the answer to complete it by adding the support.

> Describe two features of mutual self-help organisations in Notting Hill. (4 marks)

> Mutual self-help organisations were set up to help migrant families with childcare. Members of the migrant community were also helped to buy their own home.

The utility question

Look at the two sources, the exam-style question and the two answers below. Which answer is the best answer to the question, and why? You could look at page 42 for guidance on how to answer the utility question to help you make your judgement.

> How useful are Sources A and B for an enquiry into the influence of Caribbean culture on Notting Hill? (8 marks)

SOURCE A

Frank Crichlow in his Mangrove restaurant in Notting Hill, photographed by George W Hales in 1969.

SOURCE B

Johnny Edgecombe was a petty criminal in Notting Hill in the 1960s. He described his shebeen in his book *Black Scandal*, published in 2002.

There was a front room where you could listen to the latest sounds … In this room was a bar, where we served any type of drink you wanted. Next door in the bedroom was the casino … where people sat and played poker … In the front room would be some nice jazz going down, with people drinking and smoking dope. I would roll joints myself, and sell them for five shillings a spliff. While the men were gambling, the chicks sat around getting stoned and drunk.

Answer 1

Source A is useful for an enquiry into the influence of Caribbean culture on Notting Hill because it shows us Frank Crichlow, a Caribbean migrant, opening a restaurant in Notting Hill. This suggests that the migrants were able to buy businesses in the area. Source B is useful for an enquiry into the influence of Caribbean culture on Notting Hill because it describes one person's shebeen. This description suggests that Caribbean migrants provided the community with places to listen to jazz music. They were also able to go to these places to smoke and drink alcohol.

Answer 2

Source A is useful for an enquiry into the influence of Caribbean culture on Notting Hill because it shows us Frank Crichlow, a Caribbean migrant, opening a restaurant in Notting Hill. This suggests that the migrants were able to buy businesses in the area and sell Caribbean food containing spices such as thyme and tabasco sauce. Source B is useful for an enquiry into the influence of Caribbean culture on Notting Hill because it describes one person's shebeen. This description suggests that Caribbean migrants provided the community with places to listen to jazz music. They were also able to go to these places to smoke and drink alcohol. The shebeens were often in homes and in abandoned buildings. They were often the target of police raids because they sold alcohol illegally.

Which answer is better?

_____

Why?

_____

33

3 Racism and policing

3.1 The Notting Hill riots (1958)

REVISED ●

Tension had been building in Notting Hill for years due to racism and anti-immigrant groups. Some Caribbean migrants had been attacked by white youths.

The trigger to the Notting Hill riots was a fight that broke out on 29 August when a mixed-race couple suffered some racist abuse from white people outside a pub. On the night of 30 August, a group of white people attacked the home of Caribbean people. This was followed by a further six nights of attacks with petrol bombs, iron bars and knives. Some black people counter-attacked to defend their homes. As the violence got worse, the police denied that race was the cause of the riots.

After the riots, 108 people were arrested. The majority of those arrested were white people. The magistrates' courts issued fines and prison sentences ranging from a few weeks to several months. Nine youths, who were part of the Teddy Boys, were arrested before the riots and pleaded guilty to wounding and actual bodily harm. They were sentenced to four years' imprisonment. The British public were shocked by the race riots. Some newspapers blamed black people in the community. Another consequence of the violence was that black activism increased. Relations in Notting Hill worsened as black people argued they were victims of attacks and the police denied racism was a problem.

> **Key term**
>
> **Teddy Boys** A group of British youths who wore Edwardian clothes and were interested in rock n roll music. Their behaviour was sometimes rough and aggressive

3.2 The murder of Kelso Cochrane

REVISED ●

In 1959, Kelso Cochrane was stabbed, and killed, by a group of white youths. His murder received national attention. Arrests were made but the suspects were released, and nobody was ever charged with the murder. Black people were angry because they felt the police focused on claiming there was no racial motive rather than capturing the killers. Most newspapers followed by reporting that the murder was not a result of racism.

The murder of Kelso Cochrane led to a growth in civil rights and opposition to racism. Black people responded in the following ways:
+ There was a growth in black organisations to promote civil rights. The West Indian Standing Conference (WISC) was formed after the riots and was active for the next 50 years.
+ In June 1959, a 12-hour demonstration took place on Whitehall to protest about the colour bar.
+ Over one thousand people, both black and white, attended Cochrane's funeral, including Claudia Jones, who formed the Inter-Racial Friendship Coordinating Council and wrote to the Prime Minister asking him to make racially motivated violence a crime. This was without immediate success.

> **Key individuals**
>
> **Kelso Cochrane** Born in Antigua, Cochrane was a carpenter who had lived in Notting Hill since 1954. He was working to save money and study law when he was murdered aged 32
>
> **Oswald Mosley** In the 1930s, Mosley had founded the British Union of Fascists. After being released from prison, he formed the Union Movement. He claimed that black migrants were criminals and rapists

3.3 The impact of anti-immigrant groups

REVISED ●

Notting Hill in the 1950s saw several anti-immigrant groups. These groups were racist, violent and filled black people with fear because they did not feel protected by the police.
+ Teddy Boys formed gangs who attacked black people.
+ The White Defence League (WDL) campaigned violently against black migrants.
+ Oswald Mosley led a far-right political group called the Union Movement. Mosley and the party encouraged attacks on black people in Notting Hill from 1958. In 1959, he stood for Parliament in Kensington North (which included Notting Hill). Mosley suffered a humiliating defeat with only eight per cent of the votes and the Union Movement never recovered.

> **Exam tip**
>
> When you read sources about racism and policing in Notting Hill, think carefully about the motive, emotions and views of the author. How could this affect the utility of the source?

Organising knowledge

Copy the table below. Use the information on page 34 and your own knowledge to complete it with details of the causes, events and results of the two key events in Notting Hill.

	The Notting Hill riots (1958)	The murder of Kelso Cochrane (1959)
Causes		
Events		
Results		

The utility question

Look at the two sources and the exam-style question below. An answer paragraph for Source A has been written for you.

1 Using three colours, highlight where the student has used content, own knowledge and provenance to analyse the utility of the source.

2 In the space provided, complete the answer for Source B. You can also look at page 42 for guidance on how to answer the utility question.

How useful are Sources A and B for an enquiry into the Notting Hill riots (1958)? (8 marks)

SOURCE A

London police search a young black man in Talbot Road, Notting Hill, during the riots, 3 September 1958.

SOURCE B

Extract from an interview with residents of Notting Hill and a representative of the Trades Union Congress, 5 September 1958.

The most disturbing [absorbing] feature of the conversation was that the Jamaicans did not believe that if they stayed at home they would be left in peace, since a bomb had been thrown through the window of the Calypso Club in Notting Hill last Tuesday (a further incident of this kind was reported in the press on Friday), nor did they believe that the police could or would give them adequate protection. They said that police had used foul language to them particularly in the Harrow Road Police Station. The restaurant owner said that the only harm that had been done to his premises was that after the police had dispersed a threatening crowd they had come in to search for weapons and had kicked the door down so that it would not now shut. After the first incidents he had gone out to the pub to see whether the attitude towards coloured people had changed in there, but found that it had not and everyone was still friendly.

Answer

Source A is useful for an enquiry into the Notting Hill riots (1958) because it shows the reaction of the police towards the Caribbean migrant community. We can see a black youth being held and searched by the police. This is useful because it suggests that the police did not see black people as victims of the attacks, but rather as participants in the violence. Despite this, after nearly a week of violence, the majority of the 108 arrested were white people. Nevertheless, some newspapers continued to blame black people. Source A is a photograph taken on the night of 3 September, making it useful for this enquiry because it captures a search during the riots as they took place and is unlikely to have been staged due to the escalating violence taking place around this incident.

Source B is also useful for an enquiry into the Notting Hill riots (1958) because …

Exam tip

When you are explaining how a source is useful for the enquiry, it is important to develop your argument with your own knowledge.

4 Black activism in the Notting Hill area

4.1 Claudia Jones and the *West Indian Gazette*

REVISED

In 1958, Claudia Jones set up Britain's first major black-owned newspaper called the *West Indian Gazette*. This shared news, jobs and events with black people in London. Before this newspaper, there was no opportunity for the community to share information about issues that related to their lives.

4.2 The Caribbean Carnival (1959)

REVISED

Claudia Jones wanted to celebrate African-Caribbean culture and unite the community after the Notting Hill riots. The first carnival took place outside of Notting Hill in January 1959 and was sponsored by the *West Indian Gazette*. The carnival was televised by the BBC. Some of the money raised was used to help pay for the bail of black men wrongly arrested by the police. The carnival took place annually until Jones died in 1964.

From 1966, Rhaune Laslett (President of the London Free School) used the network of artists formed by Jones to develop the Notting Hill Carnival. This has continued to take place every summer into the twenty-first century and it has become the biggest street festival in Europe.

4.3 Frank Crichlow and the Mangrove restaurant

REVISED

The Mangrove restaurant served Caribbean food. Celebrities visited when in London, including Muhammad Ali, Bob Marley, Nina Simone and Marvin Gaye. The British Black Panthers frequently met here, and support was offered to black people in the community. The police frequently raided the restaurant claiming to look for drugs, but they never found any.

4.4 The British Black Panthers

REVISED

In 1968, the British Black Panthers (BBP) were founded. They campaigned for civil rights and against police brutality. Inspired by the American movement, they created pride within black people in the community by educating the people about their history and helping them to find better jobs, housing and healthcare. Their leaders included Darcus Howe and Altheia Jones-LeCointe.

4.5 The 'Mangrove Nine'

REVISED

In August 1970, a march was organised to protest about the police harassment of the Mangrove restaurant. The BBP helped to organise this march and over 150 people took part. The police arrested several people including Frank Crichlow, Darcus Howe and Altheia Jones-LeCointe, claiming that they were inciting racial violence.

+ Nine of the marchers were charged with inciting a riot. They became known as the 'Mangrove Nine'.
+ Their trial took place at the Old Bailey, the London court where the most serious crimes are heard. It attracted huge media coverage.
+ During the trial, the defendants argued that the jury should be black 'as their peers'. However, only two black jurors were selected.
+ Howe and Jones-LeCointe defended themselves.
+ The trial focused on the police brutality and racism. It showed the Mangrove Nine as victims.
+ All defendants were acquitted of the most serious charges. Four of the Mangrove Nine were given suspended sentences for minor offences.

Key individuals

Claudia Jones A black migrant from Trinidad who had been active in radical politics. She campaigned for black people to get promoted jobs, such as inspectors, in London Transport and in other organisations where there was a colour bar. She campaigned against the 1962 Commonwealth Immigrants Act (see page 27)

Frank Crichlow A migrant from Trinidad who opened the Mangrove restaurant on All Saints Road in Notting Hill

+ The judge stated that there was 'racial hatred on both sides', admitting that there was racism in the police. This made the trial a significant achievement in black British civil rights and inspired further activism.

Complete the answer

Describe two features of the British Black Panther Party. (4 marks)

Here is the first part of an answer to this question.

> Feature 1:
>
> *The British Black Panther Party wanted to help black people in Notting Hill to feel pride in themselves. They did this by educating them about black history.*

1 Highlight the following:
   + Where the feature has been identified.
   + Where supporting information has been added.
2 Now add a second feature.

Feature 2:

_____

_____

The follow-up question

Look at the source and exam-style question below. Select a detail from the source and write a follow-up question in the table.

How could you follow up Source B to find out more about the 1959 Caribbean Carnival?

SOURCE B

Extracts from the message published by Claudia Jones in the souvenir brochure for the Caribbean Carnival (1959).

Rarely have the energies of a people indigenous to another homeland been so quickly and spontaneously generated to such purpose as witness the work of the Caribbean Carnival Committee 1959, … A pride in being West Indian is undoubtedly at the root of this unity: a pride that has its origin in the drama of nascent [emerging] nationhood, and that pride encompasses not only the creativeness, uniqueness and originality of West Indian mime, song and dance – but is the genesis of the nation itself … We have a determination to make the *WIG* Caribbean Carnival an annual event.

Detail in Source B that I would follow up:	
Question I would ask:	

Make a list of additional questions that you could ask from this source to find out more about the 1959 Caribbean Carnival.

Exam tip

Check that the detail you choose to follow up and the question that you ask will provide more information about the focus of the enquiry.

5 The national and regional context

5.1 Britain after the Second World War

REVISED ⬤

After the Second World War, Britain had to recover from years of fighting and the damage caused by the war.

+ Civilians had been killed in German bombing raids.
+ Cities were damaged from bombing.
+ British people were left homeless.
+ Britain was almost £21 billion in debt and had lost wealth directly linked to its Empire.

Millions of people from across the British Empire had fought for Britain in the armed forces. This included people from the Caribbean.

5.2 Reconstruction and demand for labour

REVISED ⬤

Britain needed workers to rebuild the country and support the NHS and British railways. The British Government passed the British Nationality Act (1948) with the intention of recruiting more workers from white settler families in the Commonwealth (see page 24). Many people in the Caribbean felt loyal to Britain following their connection through the British Empire. They saw Britain as 'the Mother Country'. Some saw the 1948 Act as an opportunity to find work and earn higher wages while rebuilding Britain.

Thousands of people migrated to Britain, including engineers, nurses and bus drivers. People were encouraged to migrate by the Caribbean newspapers but some in the British government tried to dissuade them. The NHS and London Transport became two of the largest employers of Caribbean migrants. However, the migrants found working in Britain difficult because of discrimination including the colour bar and lower wages.

5.3 The 'Swinging Sixties'

REVISED ⬤

Things had improved in Britain by the 1960s. People had found employment and rationing was ending. This led to a greater amount of freedom and the decade became known as the 'Swinging Sixties'. London was an exciting city and a centre for music, fashion and political activism. However, it is important to remember that black people still experienced inequality and racism.

5.4 Poverty in London

REVISED ⬤

Caribbean migrants were shocked by the poverty in London, which included:

+ the rationing of goods, including electricity, bread and fabric
+ housing shortages
+ bomb damage.

5.5 Policing in London

REVISED ⬤

London had the Metropolitan Police Force. In the 1950s, most officers were white males. Black people who tried to join the police force were refused. Many police officers held racist views and did little to build a relationship with black people. These views continued during this period because there were no laws against racial discrimination or harassment. This led to distrust between black residents of areas such as Notting Hill and the police force.

Key term

Rationing A government policy that fixed the amount people could buy of food and household goods. This was to ensure there was enough for everyone

Revision activity

Look back at what you have learned about migration in the years c.1900 to the present day. How much of the reasons for migration, and the experiences and impact of migrants, can be seen in the study of Notting Hill between c.1948 and c.1970?

Organising knowledge

Look back over the information on pages 30–32, 34 and 36–38. Make a copy of the table below. Complete it to categorise migration in Notting Hill in the years c.1948 to c.1970.

Caribbean migrants in Notting Hill		
Reasons for migration and settlement	**Experience of migrants**	**Impact of migrants**

Organising knowledge

Study the different types of sources available to a historian when enquiring into Notting Hill in the years c.1948 to c.1970 in the table below. Complete the table. For each type of source explain what aspects of Notting Hill covered in this book it would be useful for, and explain the advantages of using it. For example, census data would be useful in providing information about residents in a property including names, ages and occupations. This information would not have been produced for propaganda and so would give the historian reliable, accurate information.

Types of sources	Useful for …	Advantages
National newspapers		
Photographs		
Government records		
Census data		
Opinion polls		
Television reports		
Local newspapers		
Publications written for the Caribbean community		
Local council and police records		
Housing and employment records		
Oral and written memoirs of local residents		

39

Exam focus

Your History GCSE is made up of three exams:

+ In Paper 1 you have one hour and 15 minutes to answer questions on a thematic study and historic environment, in your case Migrants in Britain, c.800–present and Notting Hill c.1948–c.1970.
+ In Paper 2 you have one hour and 45 minutes to answer questions on a period study and a British depth study.
+ In Paper 3 you have one hour and 20 minutes to answer questions on a modern depth study.

For Paper 1 you have to answer the following types of questions. Each requires you to demonstrate different historical skills:

+ **Question 1** is a key features question in which you have to describe two features and characteristics of the period.

+ **Question 2** includes two sub-questions on a source enquiry which test your source analysis skills as well as your ability to frame a historical question.
+ **Question 3** is a key features question in which you have to describe the similarity or difference for migrants in Britain between two time periods.
+ **Question 4** is a causation question which asks you to explain why there was change in an aspect of the history of migration.
+ **Questions 5 and 6** are analytical questions that ask you to evaluate change, continuity and significance in migration.

The table below gives a summary of the question types for Paper 1 and what you need to do.

Question number	Marks	Key words	You need to …
1	4	Describe two features of …	+ Identify two features + Add supporting information for each feature
2(a)	8	How useful are Sources A and B for an enquiry into …? Explain your answer, using Sources A and B and your knowledge of the historical context.	+ Ensure that you explain the value of the contents of each of the sources + Explain how the provenance of each source affects the value of the contents + Support your answer with your knowledge of the given topic
2(b)	4	How could you follow up Source B to find out more about … In your answer you must give the question you would ask and the type of source you could use.	+ Select a detail from Source B that could form the basis of a follow-up enquiry + Write a question that is linked to this detail and enquiry + Identify an appropriate type of source for the enquiry + Explain how the type of source might help answer your follow-up question
3	4	Explain one way in which … were similar/different in the … and … centuries.	+ Identify a similarity or difference + Support the comparison with specific detail from both periods
4	12	Explain why … You may use the following in your answer: [two given points] You **must** also use information of your own.	+ Explain at least three causes of change – you can use the points in the question but must also use at least one point of your own + Ensure that you focus the causes on the question
5/6	20	'Statement'. How far do you agree? Explain your answer. You may use the following in your answer: [two given points] You **must** also use information of your own.	+ Ensure you agree and disagree with the statement + Use the given points and your own knowledge + Ensure you write a conclusion giving your final judgement on the question + There are up to 4 marks for spelling, punctuation, grammar and the use of specialist terminology.

Check your understanding and progress at **www.hoddereducation.co.uk/myrevisionnotes**

Question 1: Key features

Below is an example of a key features question which is worth 4 marks.

> Describe **two** features of the Mangrove restaurant.

Feature 1: _____

_____

Feature 2: _____

_____

How to answer

You have to identify two features and add supporting information for each. For each of the two features you are given space to write. Remember you need to identify **two** different features. Below is a sample answer to this inference question with comments around it.

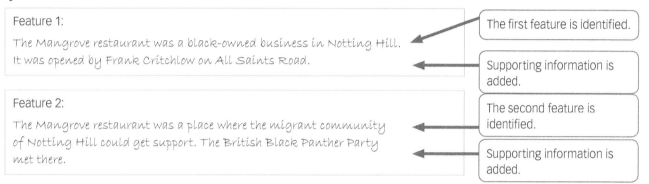

Feature 1:

The Mangrove restaurant was a black-owned business in Notting Hill. It was opened by Frank Critchlow on All Saints Road.

> The first feature is identified.

> Supporting information is added.

Feature 2:

The Mangrove restaurant was a place where the migrant community of Notting Hill could get support. The British Black Panther Party met there.

> The second feature is identified.

> Supporting information is added.

Complete the answer

> Describe two features of the development of All Saints Road.

Here is the first part of an answer to this question.

Feature 1:

All Saints Road became the centre of black people in the community in the 1950s. Shops and restaurants owned by Caribbean migrants opened on All Saints Road.

1 Highlight the following:
   + Where the feature has been identified.
   + Where supporting information has been added.
2 Now add a second feature.

Feature 2: _____

_____

Question 2: Source analysis

Question 2 is divided into two parts.
+ Question 2(a) is a utility question on two sources. You have to explain how useful each source is to a historical enquiry.
+ Question 2(b) is an analysis question that asks you to use sources. You have to explain a follow-up enquiry and the source that you would use.

Question 2(a): Utility

Below is an example of a utility question which is worth 8 marks. The sources will be labelled Source A and Source B.

> Study Sources A and B. How useful are Sources A and B for an enquiry into the problems of housing in Notting Hill? Explain your answer, using Sources A and B and your own knowledge of the historical context. **(8 marks)**

> a) What does Stead suggest had happened in Rachman's Notting Hill properties after he died?
>
> b) How does Stead present Peter Rachman's legacy?

SOURCE A

A photograph of Silchester Road, Notting Hill, 1967.

SOURCE B

An article in *The Guardian* newspaper by Jean Stead published on 6 August 1963.

The new committee say the same men with their heavy-glove accomplices are still collecting the rents today, even though Rachman has gone, and the landlords' names have changed. The rent agents' methods remain the same. Families are still put forcibly onto the street, tenants are still terrorised out by a variety of legal and illegal methods … The choice for the tenants is always overcrowding and high rents or the streets. In these circumstances, the human choice is to settle for the evil you know.

How to answer

REVISED ○

- ✦ Write two paragraphs, one for each source.
- ✦ Explain how the content of each source is useful for the enquiry.

- ✦ Explain how the provenance of each source is useful for the enquiry. Think: nature, origin OR purpose.
- ✦ Add some contextual knowledge to develop your points about content and/or provenance.

> **Provenance** Who wrote or created the source, when and for what purpose. This can have a big impact on what the source tells us

Below is part of a sample Level 3 answer to this question in which is explained the utility of Source A. Read it and the comments around it.

> Source A is useful because it shows the poor housing conditions in Notting Hill. In the photo we can see that the house has been neglected because the windows are smashed and there is lots of waste outside the front of the house. Landlords struggled to rent out these houses and so accepted Caribbean migrants as tenants. The migrants had no choice but to rent these properties because most landlords would not rent their properties to them because of the colour of their skin. The Caribbean migrants were taken advantage of and charged high rents for the poor housing. The usefulness of Source A is further enhanced by its provenance. This source is a photograph and this makes it useful for the enquiry because it is a snapshot in time and will show the reality of the conditions of the housing in Notting Hill.

A judgement is made on the value of the content of the source.

Own knowledge is used to support this judgement.

The provenance of the source is taken into account when making a judgement on its utility.

Analysing utility

Now write your own Level 3 answer on Source B. Remember to take into account how the provenance affects the usefulness of the source content.

Question 2(b): Framing a historical question

Below is an example of a source question requiring you to frame an enquiry. This is worth 4 marks.

> How could you follow up Source B to find out more about the problems of housing in Notting Hill? In your answer, you must give the question you would ask and the type of source you could use.

How to answer

You have to identify a follow-up enquiry and explain how you would carry this out. For each of the questions you are given space to write. Below is a sample answer to this question with comments around it.

Detail in Source B that I would follow up:

"The choice for the tenants is always overcrowding and high rents or the streets."

→ The follow-up enquiry is identified.

Question I would ask:

On average, how many families lived in one rental property in Notting Hill?

→ The linked question is asked.

What type of source I could use:

1961 census data of Notting Hill.

→ An appropriate source is identified.

How this might help answer my question:

The 1961 census data will tell us how many families, and people, were recorded living in the rental properties in Notting Hill.

→ An explanation of how the source would help with the follow-up enquiry.

Question 3: Similarity or difference

Below is an example of a key features question which is worth 4 marks.

> Explain **one** way in which the impact of migrants in England was similar in the years c.1500–c.1700 to the impact of migrants in Britain in the years c.1700–c.1900.

How to answer

+ Explain the similarity between the two time periods.

+ Use specific information from both time periods to support the comparison, showing good knowledge and understanding.

Below is a sample answer to this with comments around it.

In the years c.1500–c.1700 migrants in England had a large impact on trade. The cloth trade benefited from the skills of the Huguenots as England's silk production increased and was exported overseas. Similarly, in the years c.1700–c.1900 migrants in Britain had an impact on trade. The canals and railways built by Irish and Italian navvies led to the movement of raw materials and finished goods around Britain and to ports to be transported overseas.

→ The impact of migrants in the years c.1500–c.1700 is identified.

→ Own knowledge is used to support this.

→ The similar impact of migrants in the years c.1700–c.1900 is identified.

→ Own knowledge is used to support this.

Develop the detail

Below is a question and part of an answer. Read the answer and develop the detail.

> Explain **one** way in which reasons for migration to England were different in the years c.800–c.1500 to the reasons for migration to Britain in the years c.1900–present.

> In the years c.800–c.1500 people migrated to England for land. However, during the years c.1900–present people have migrated to Britain as refugees to escape persecution.

Question 4: Causation

Below is an example of a causation question which is worth 12 marks.

> Explain why the experiences of migrants in Britain changed in the years c.1900 to the present day.

You may use the following in your answer:
+ Anti-immigration movements
+ Asian migrants in Leicester from 1945

You **must** also include information of your own.

How to answer

REVISED ●

+ You need to explain change or continuity with reasons/causes that are fully focused on the question.
+ Support your answer with at least three features of knowledge. This could be the two mentioned in the bullet points and one of your own. You don't have to use the bullet points; you could decide to use different features of your own knowledge instead.

Below is part of an answer to the question.

> Political parties were formed after c.1900 to oppose immigration, including the National Front and the British National Party. In 1968, Enoch Powell (Conservative MP for Wolverhampton) made his 'Rivers of Blood' speech. Some British people marched in support of him. Equal rights movements were also formed by migrants throughout the twentieth century. These included the League of Coloured People in London and the West African Students' Union. Following the Race Relations Acts the experiences of migrants in Britain changed.

> Anti-immigration movements are described. However, there is no explicit focus on the question.

> The supporting evidence is not precise enough.

> The answer is losing focus on the question.

Make an improvement

Try improving the answer.

An example of a better answer to this question is on page 45 for you to check your own answer against.

Exam tip

Writing a good paragraph to explain an answer to something is as easy as PEEing – Point, Example, Explain.

Your point is a short answer to the question. You then back this up with lots of examples to demonstrate all the knowledge you have learned during your studies: this is the section that proves you have studied and revised, rather than just guessing. Finally, you will link that knowledge to the question by explaining in a final sentence.

+ Point: Passing my GCSE History exam will be very helpful in the future.
+ Example: For example, it will help me to continue my studies next year.
+ Explain: This will help me to get the job I want in the future.

Check your understanding and progress at **www.hoddereducation.co.uk/myrevisionnotes**

Below is a sample answer to the causation question on page 44 with comments around it.

The experiences of migrants changed in the years c.1900 to present because of the increase in support for anti-immigration in Britain, especially in British politics. Political parties were formed to oppose immigration, including the National Front in 1967 and the British National Party in 1982. In 1968, Enoch Powell (Conservative MP for Wolverhampton) made his 'Rivers of Blood' speech. Some British people marched in support of him, including London dock workers. A survey reported that 75 per cent of British people believed there were too many minority ethnic migrants living in Britain. This led to a change in the experiences of migrants in Britain because the support for anti-immigration politics increased the amount of discrimination, racism and violence they experienced. Those who attacked migrants felt they were supported by people in authority, and this only encouraged their behaviour further.

> The first cause is introduced and immediately focuses on the question.

> The supporting evidence is precise and relevant to the question.

The experiences of Asian migrants in Leicester also changed in the years following 1945 because of support for anti-immigration movements from the existing population. Many Asian migrants were attracted to the existing migrant community in Leicester after 1945. The National Front protested in Leicester with marches in 1974 and 1979. However, the support for this anti-immigration movement did not last throughout the period. Following support in the 1970s, its popularity declined in the 1980s due to its racism and violence. This led to an improvement in the experiences of Asian migrants in Leicester because they did not have to experience the discrimination as frequently or violence as intensely.

> The second cause is introduced and linked to the first cause and immediately focuses on the question.

> The supporting evidence is precise and relevant to the question.

The experience of migrants in Britain since c.1900 has improved because of key legislation from the government. The Race Relations Act was passed in 1965, with further legislation in 1968 and 1976. These laws were passed by Parliament to end the discrimination that migrant communities faced and to ensure they were treated equally to white people. Legislation, including the Race Relations Acts, changed the experiences of migrants in Britain because they were now protected by law from discrimination, racism and violence. Previously this behaviour had gone unchecked, leading to discrimination in many areas of their daily lives including housing, employment and education.

> The third cause is introduced and immediately focuses on the question.

> The supporting evidence is precise and relevant to the question. Notice that this feature of knowledge is not listed in the bullet points.

Now have a go

Explain why migration to England increased in the years c.1500–c.1700.

You may use the following in your answer:
+ Global trading companies
+ Huguenots

You **must** also use information of your own.

Question 5 and 6: A judgement about change, continuity and significance

Below is an example of question 5 and 6, which ask you to make a judgement about how far you agree with the statement. They are worth 20 marks (4 of these are for spelling, punctuation, grammar and the use of specialist terminology).

> 'There was little change in the impact migrants had in Britain in the years c.1500 to c.1900.' How far do you agree? Explain your answer.

You may use the following in your answer.
+ Huguenots
+ Politics

You **must** also include information of your own.

How to answer

REVISED ●

You need to give a balanced answer which agrees and disagrees with the statement using supporting information from the bullet points as well as information from your own knowledge. Here is one way you could approach this:
+ Agree with the view and support this with information from one bullet point and your own knowledge.
+ Disagree with the view and support this with information from one bullet point and your own knowledge.
+ Make a final judgement on how far you agree or disagree with the statement.

Below is part of an answer to this question which agrees with the view given in the statement.

It can be argued that there was little change in the impact of migrants in Britain in the years c.1500 to c.1900 because throughout this period they continued to have an impact on trade. During seventeenth-century England, Huguenots in England helped to develop the silk weaving industry. They shared their expertise and experience with the local community. English weavers learned techniques from the Huguenots, including taffetas and brocades. England's silk production increased and was exported abroad. There was a high demand for silk woven by the Huguenots from overseas. Migrants in Britain continued to have an impact on trade as Britain industrialised in the eighteenth and nineteenth centuries. The Irish and Italian navvies worked to build the canals and railways that enabled the movement of raw materials, such as cotton, from the docks in Liverpool to factories in Manchester. Once in factories, these materials were manufactured into finished goods and then traded within and beyond Britain. Without the contributions and hard work of the Irish and Italian migrants, Britain would not have been able to trade goods and prosper so much during the nineteenth century. This shows that there was little change in the impact of migrants in Britain between c.1500 and c.1900 because they continued to have an impact on trade, either by sharing their skills to benefit Britain or by building the transport networks to allow Britain to trade.

> The answer immediately focuses on the question.

> Support is provided using the first bullet point and information from own knowledge.

> Explanation is provided.

Now have a go

1 Have a go at another paragraph by disagreeing with the view given in the statement.
2 Support this with information using the second bullet point and your own knowledge.
3 Write a conclusion giving your final judgement on the question.

Check your understanding and progress at **www.hoddereducation.co.uk/myrevisionnotes**